Woven Beanie	30	Heige Hat	32	Two Color Slouch Hat	34	Junior Crocheted Hat	36
Pennington Hat	37	Wave Pattern Hat and Cowl	38	The Casual Friday Hat	40	Next Generation Hat	42
Town and Country Hat	44	Iconic Hat	46	Ridgewood Hat	47	Greenpoint Grunge Cap	48
Hat and Mitts	50	Slouchy Stripe Hat	52	The Romantic Hat	54	First Fall Crochet Hat	56
Urban Minimalist Hat	57	Warmest Regards Hat	58	Toboggan Hat	60	Simply Basic Hat, Scarf, and Gloves Set	62

Two Color Hat and Tied Scarf

Easy

MEASUREMENTS

HAT
Finished Circumference About 19"/48.5cm*
*Will stretch to fit a range of sizes.

SCARF
Triangle length About 12"/30.5cm
Tie length 50"/127cm

MATERIALS

YARN
LION BRAND® Jeans®, 3½oz/100g balls, each approx 246yd/225m (acrylic)
- 1 ball each in #105 Faded (A) and #109 Stonewash (B)

HOOK
- One size H-8 (5mm) crochet hook, *or size to obtain gauge*

NOTIONS
- Stitch markers
- Pompom maker
- Tapestry needle

GAUGE
17 sc-blo + 17 rows = about 4"/10cm.
BE SURE TO CHECK YOUR GAUGE.

STITCH GLOSSARY
sc-blo (sc in back loop only) Insert hook in back loop only of indicated st and draw up a loop, yarn over and draw through 2 loops on hook.

sc2tog-blo (sc 2 sts tog in back loops only) [Insert hook in back loop only of next st and draw up a loop] twice, yarn over and draw through all 3 loops on hook —1 st decreased.

NOTES
1) Scarf is worked in 2 steps with 2 colors of yarn. First a tie is worked back and forth in rows. Then, stitches are worked along one long edge of tie to begin the triangle section.

2) Hat is worked in 2 steps with 2 colors of yarn. First the Hat is worked back and forth in rows. Then, stitches are worked across one long edge of the Hat to begin the lower band. Hat is then sewn together and a pom-pom is tied on.

3) To change yarn color, work last st of old color to last yarn over. Yarn over with new color and draw through all loops on hook to complete st. Proceed with new color.

4) Diagrams are provided to clarify the construction of the Hat and Scarf.

SCARF

TIE
With A, ch 11.
Row 1 Sc in 2nd ch from hook and in each ch across— you will have 10 sc at the end of Row 1.
Row 2 Ch 1, turn, sc in first st, sc-blo in each st to last st, sc in last st.
Rep Row 2 until piece measures about 25"/63.5cm from beg, change to B in last st of last row.
Fasten off A.
With B, rep Row 2 until piece measures about 50"/127cm from beg. Fasten off.

TRIANGLE
Note When changing yarn color, do not fasten off old color until instructed. Drop old color to back of piece and pick it up again when next needed.
Place tie onto a flat surface with one long edge at top, A-colored half to your right and B-colored half to your

left (if you crochet left-handed, place A-colored half to your left and B-colored half to your right).

Place 2 markers on top edge, each about 8"/20cm from center of tie (color change is center of tie).

Row 1 From RS, join B with a sl st at first marker (in A-colored section), ch 1, work 33 sc evenly spaced along edge to center of tie; change to A and work 33 sc evenly spaced along edge to 2nd marker—66 sc. Remove markers.

Dec Row 2 With A, ch 1, turn, sc in first st, sc2tog-blo, sc-blo in each st to center; change to B, sc-blo in each st to last 3 sts, sc2tog-blo, sc in last st—64 sc.

Dec Row 3 With B, ch 1, turn, sc in first st, sc2tog-blo, sc-blo in each st to center; change to A, sc-blo in each st to last 3 sts, sc2tog-blo, sc in last st—62 sc.

Dec Row 4 With A, ch 1, turn, sc in first st, sc2tog-blo, sc-blo in each st to center; change to B, sc-blo in each st to last 3 sts, sc2tog-blo, sc in last st—60 sc.

Row 5 With B, ch 1, turn, sc in first st, sc-blo in each st to center; change to A, sc-blo in each st to last st, sc in last st.

Rows 6–41 Rep Rows 2–5 nine more times—6 sc.

Row 42 Rep Row 2—4 sc.

Row 43 With B, ch 1, turn, sc2tog-blo; change to A, sc2tog-blo—2 sc.

Row 44 With A, ch 1, turn, sc2tog-blo—1 sc.

Fasten off.

FINISHING
Weave in ends.

HAT
With A, ch 31.

Row 1 With A, sc in 2nd ch from hook and in each ch across—30 sc.

Two Color Hat and Tied Scarf

Rows 2–40 With A, ch 1, turn, sc in first st, sc-blo in each st to last st, sc in last st. Change to B in last st of last row. Fasten off A.

Rows 41–80 With B, ch 1, turn, sc in first st, sc-blo in each st to last st, sc in last st. Do NOT fasten off.

BAND

Row 1 (RS) With B, ch 1, do not turn, work 80 sc evenly spaced in ends of rows along side edge—80 sc.

Rows 2–9 Ch 1, turn, sc in first st, sc-blo in each st to last st, sc in last st.

Fasten off, leaving a long yarn tail for sewing.

FINISHING

With yarn tail, sew edges of band tog, then sew first and last rows of Hat tog.

Thread yarn tail in and out through ends of rows around top of Hat. Pull yarn tail to close opening at top of Hat and knot securely.

Pompom

With A, and following package directions, make a medium size pompom.

Tie pompom to Hat.

Weave in ends. •

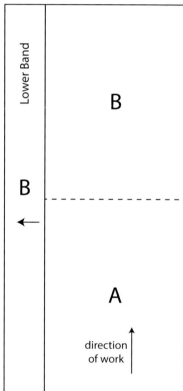

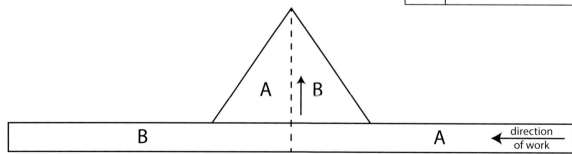

I Wanna Crochet a Hat

Easy

MEASUREMENTS
Finished Circumference About 20"/51cm*
*Hat will stretch to fit a range of sizes.
Finished Height About 8½"/21.5cm

MATERIALS
YARN
LION BRAND® Wool-Ease® Thick & Quick®, 6oz/170g balls, each approx 106yd/97m (acrylic/wool)
- 1 ball each in #536 Fossil (A), #99 Fisherman (B), and #124 Barley (C)

HOOK
- One size N (10mm) crochet hook, *or size to obtain gauge*

NOTIONS
- Stitch markers
- Tapestry needle
- Large pompom maker

GAUGE
7 sc = about 4"/10cm.
BE SURE TO CHECK YOUR GAUGE.

NOTES
1) The Hat is worked in one piece in the round and beginning at top, with the RS always facing.
2) To change color, work last stitch of old color to last yarn over. Yarn over with new color and draw through all loops to complete stitch. Fasten off old color.

HAT
With A, ch 2.
Rnd 1 Work 6 sc in 2nd ch from hook.
Place marker for beg of rnd, move marker up as each rnd is completed.
Rnd 2 Work 2 sc in each st around—you'll have 12 sc.
Rnd 3 *Sc in next sc, 2 sc in next sc; rep from * around—18 sc.
Rnd 4 *Sc in next 2 sc, 2 sc in next sc; rep from * around—24 sc.
Rnd 5 *Sc in next 3 sc, 2 sc in next sc; rep from * around—30 sc.
Rnd 6 *Sc in next 4 sc, 2 sc in next sc; rep from * around—36 sc.
Rnds 7–11 Sc around, changing to B in last st of Rnd 11.
Rnd 12 With B, rep Rnd 7, changing to C in last st.
Rnds 13–16 With C, rep Rnd 7.
Fasten off.

FINISHING
With B and large pompom maker, make a pompom. Tie pom-pom to Hat. •

Perfectly Simple Crochet Hat

Easy

SIZES
Child S (Child M/L, Adult S/M, Adult L)

MEASUREMENTS
Finished Circumference About 16 (18½, 21, 22)"/40.5 (47, 53.5, 56)cm*
*Will stretch to fit a range of sizes.

MATERIALS
YARN
LION BRAND® Wool-Ease® Thick & Quick®, 6oz/170g balls, each approx 106yd/97m (acrylic/wool)
- 1 ball in #149 Charcoal

HOOK
- One size N-13 (9mm) crochet hook, *or size to obtain gauge*

NOTIONS
- Stitch markers
- Tapestry needle

GAUGE
6½ sc = 4"/10cm.
BE SURE TO CHECK YOUR GAUGE.

STITCH GLOSSARY
FPDC (front post double crochet) Yarn over, insert hook from front to back then to front, going around post of indicated st, draw up a loop, [yarn over and draw through 2 loops on hook] twice. Skip st behind the FPDC.

NOTES
1) Band is worked in the rnd with RS always facing, do not turn.

2) Hat is worked in rnds, turning at the end of every rnd.

HAT
BAND
Ch 26 (30, 34, 36). Being careful not to twist, join with sl st in first ch to make a ring.
Rnd 1 Ch 2 (counts as first hdc), hdc in next ch and in each ch around; join with sl st in top of beg ch-2. Place marker for beg of rnd, move marker up as each rnd is completed—26 (30, 34, 36) sts.
Rnd 2 Ch 2 (counts as first hdc), *FPDC in next st, hdc in next st; rep from * to last st, FPDC in last st, join with sl st to top of beg ch-2.

Adult sizes only
Rnd 3 Rep Rnd 2.

BODY
Rnd 1 Ch 1, sc into each st around.
Rnd 2 Ch 1, turn. Working into sps between sts, sc into each sp around, join with sl st in beg ch.
Rep Rnd 2 until 7 (7, 8, 9) rnds have been completed.

SHAPE CROWN
Dec Rnd 1 Ch 1, turn. Working into sps between sts, *sc2tog, sc into next 3 sps; rep from * 4 (4, 5, 5) more times, sc in each sp to end of rnd, join with sl st in beg ch—21 (25, 28, 30) sts.
Dec Rnd 2 Ch 1, turn. Working into sps between sts, *sc2tog, sc into next 2 sps; rep from * 4 (4, 5, 5) more times, sc into each sp to end of rnd, join with sl st in beg ch—16 (20, 22, 24) sts.
Dec Rnd 3 Ch1, turn. Working into sps between sts, *sc2tog, sc into next sp; rep from * 4 (4, 5, 5) more times, sc into each sp to end of rnd, join with sl st in beg ch—11 (15, 16, 18) sts.

Dec Rnd 4 Ch1, turn. Working into sps between sts, sc2tog to last 1 (1, 0, 0) sp, sc in next 1 (1, 0, 0) sp. Fasten off leaving a long yarn tail.
Thread tail through sts of last rnd and pull to gather. Knot securely.

FINISHING
Weave in ends. •

Rue Royale Beret

Easy

MEASUREMENTS
Finished Circumference at Lower Edge About 19"/48.5cm*
*Will stretch to fit a range of sizes.

MATERIALS
YARN
LION BRAND® Mandala Tweed Stripes®, 5.3oz/150g cakes, each approx 426yd/390m (acrylic)
• 1 ball in #220 Dragonfly

HOOK
• One size H-8 (5mm) crochet hook, *or size to obtain gauge*

NOTION
• Tapestry needle

GAUGE
15 sc = about 5"/12.5cm.
BE SURE TO CHECK YOUR GAUGE.

NOTE
The Beret is worked in one piece in joined rnds from the top downwards. The right side will always be facing.

BERET
Wrap yarn around index finger. Insert hook into ring on finger, yarn over and draw up a loop. Carefully slip ring from finger and work the stitches of Rnd 1 into the ring.
Rnd 1 Ch 1, work 6 sc in ring; join with sl st in first sc. Pull gently but firmly on tail to tighten center ring. In all following rnds work first st(s) into same sc as joining sl st.
Rnd 2 Ch 1, 2 sc in each sc around; join with sl st in first sc—you will have 12 sc in this rnd.
Rnd 3 Ch 1, *sc in next sc, 2 sc in next sc; rep from * around; join with sl st in first sc—18 sc.
Rnd 4 Ch 1, sc in first sc, *2 sc in next sc, sc in next 2 sc; rep from * to last 2 sc, 2 sc in next sc, sc in last sc; join with sl st in first sc—24 sc.
Rnd 5 Ch 1, *sc in next 3 sc, 2 sc in next sc; rep from * around; join with sl st in first sc—30 sc.
Rnd 6 Ch 1, sc in first 2 sc, *2 sc in next sc, sc in next 4 sc; rep from * to last 3 sc, 2 sc in next sc, sc in last 2 sc; join with sl st in first sc—36 sc.
Rnd 7 Ch 1, *2 sc in next sc, sc in next 5 sc; rep from * around; join with sl st in first sc—42 sc.
Rnd 8 Ch 1, sc in first 3 sc, *2 sc in next sc, sc in next 6 sc; rep from * to last 4 sc, 2 sc in next sc, sc in last 3 sc; join with sl st in first sc—48 sc.
Rnd 9 Ch 1, *2 sc in next sc, sc in next 7 sc; rep from * around; join with sl st in first sc—54 sc.
Rnd 10 Ch 1, sc in first 6 sc, *2 sc in next sc, sc in next 8 sc; rep from * to last 3 sc, 2 sc in next sc, sc in last 2 sc; join with sl st in first sc—60 sc.
Rnd 11 Ch 1, sc in first 3 sc, *2 sc in next sc, sc in next 9 sc; rep from * to last 7 sc, 2 sc in next sc, sc in last 6 sc; join with sl st in first sc—66 sc.
Rnd 12 Ch 1, *2 sc in next sc, sc in next 10 sc; rep from * around; join with sl st in first sc—72 sc.
Rnd 13 Ch 1, sc in first 7 sc, *2 sc in next sc, sc in next 11 sc; rep from * to last 5 sc, 2 sc in next sc, sc in last 4 sc; join with sl st in first sc—78 sc.
Rnd 14 Ch 1, sc in first 3 sc, *2 sc in next sc, sc in next 12 sc; rep from * to last 10 sc, 2 sc in next sc, sc in last 9 sc; join with sl st in first sc—84 sc.
Rnd 15 Ch 1, sc in first 12 sc, *2 sc in next sc, sc in next 13 sc; rep from * to last 2 sc, 2 sc in next sc, sc in last sc; join with sl st in first sc—90 sc.
Rnd 16 Ch 1, sc in first 8 sc, *2 sc in next sc, sc in next 14 sc; rep from * to last 7 sc, 2 sc in next sc, sc in last 6 sc; join with sl st in first sc—96 sc.

Rnd 17 Ch 1, *2 sc in next sc, sc in next 15 sc; rep from * around; join with sl st in first sc—102 sc.

Rnd 18 Ch 1, sc in first 5 sc, *2 sc in next sc, sc in next 16 sc; rep from * to last 12 sc, 2 sc in next sc, sc in last 11 sc; join with sl st in first sc—108 sc.

Rnds 19–24 Ch 1, sc in each sc around; join with sl st in first sc.

Rnd 25 Ch 1, sc in first 6 sc, *sc2tog, sc in next 16 sc; rep from * to last 12 sc, sc2tog, sc in last 10 sc; join with sl st in first sc—102 sc.

Rnd 26 Ch 1, sc in each sc around; join with sl st in first sc.

Rnd 27 Ch 1, *sc2tog, sc in next 15 sc; rep from * around; join with sl st in first sc—96 sc.

Rnd 28 Ch 1, sc in each sc around; join with sl st in first sc.

Rnd 29 Ch 1, sc in first 8 sc, *sc2tog, sc in next 14 sc; rep from * to last 8 sc, sc2tog, sc in last 6 sc; join with sl st in first sc—90 sc.

Rnd 30 Ch 1, *sc2tog, sc in next 13 sc; rep from * around; join with sl st in first sc—84 sc.

Rnd 31 Ch 1, sc in first 4 sc, *sc2tog, sc in next 12 sc; rep from * to last 10 sc, sc2tog, sc in last 8 sc; join with sl st in first sc—78 sc.

Rnd 32 Ch 1, *sc2tog, sc in next 9 sc; rep from * to last 12 sc, sc2tog, sc in last 10 sc; join with sl st in first sc—71 sc.

Rnds 33–35 Working in back loops only, sc in each sc around; join with sl st in first sc.

Rnd 36 Ch 1, working in back loops only, sl st in each sc around. Fasten off.

FINISHING

Weave in ends. •

Oslo Hat

Easy

MEASUREMENTS
Finished Circumference About 20"/51cm*
*Will stretch to fit a range of sizes.
Finished Height About 11"/28cm

MATERIALS
YARN
LION BRAND® Wool-Ease® Thick & Quick®, 6oz/170g balls, each approx 106yd/97m (acrylic/wool) 6
• 1 ball in #172 Kale

HOOK
• One size N-13 (9mm) crochet hook, *or size to obtain gauge*

NOTIONS
• Tapestry needle

GAUGE
8 sts + 5½ rnds = about 4"/10cm over Rnds 1–5.
BE SURE TO CHECK YOUR GAUGE.

STITCH GLOSSARY
FPDC (front post double crochet) Yarn over, insert hook from front to back then to front, going around post of indicated st, draw up a loop, [yarn over and draw through 2 loops on hook] twice. Skip st behind the FPDC.
hdc-blo (half double crochet in back loop only) Yarn over, insert hook in back loop only of indicated st and draw up a loop, yarn over and draw through all 3 loops on hook.
hdc-flo (half double crochet in front loop only) Yarn over, insert hook in front loop only of indicated st and draw up a loop, yarn over and draw through all 3 loops on hook.

NOTES
1) Hat is worked in one piece in joined and turned rnds beg at lower edge.
2) If you find it difficult to join the beg ch into a ring without twisting the ch, Rnd 1 can be worked as a row then joined into a rnd, as follows: Leaving a long beg tail, ch 41, sc in 2nd ch from hook and in each ch across; join with sl st in first sc—you will have 40 sc in this row/rnd. Use beg tail to sew gap at base of first row closed and proceed to Rnd 2.
3) When instructed to work in a st "2 rnds below", work into the indicated st in the rnd numbered 2 less than the rnd you are currently working. For example, when working Rnd 3, a st "2 rnds below" is in Rnd 3 - 2 = Rnd 1.
4) For those who find a visual helpful, we have included a stitch diagram.

HAT
Ch 40, taking care not to twist ch, join with sl st in first ch to make a ring.
Rnd 1 (RS) Ch 1, sc in same ch as join and in each ch around; join with sl st in first sc—you will have 40 sc in this rnd.
Rnd 2 Ch 2 (counts as hdc), turn, hdc in next st and in each st around; join with sl st in top of beg ch-2.
Rnd 3 Ch 1, turn, sc in same st as join, FPDC around next st 2 rnds below, *sc in next st, FPDC around next st 2 rnds below; rep from * around; join with sl st in first sc—20 sc and 20 FPDC.
Rnd 4 Ch 2 (counts as hdc), turn, hdc-flo in next st and in each st around; join with sl st in top of beg ch-2.
Rnd 5 Ch 2 (counts as hdc), turn, hdc-blo in next st and in each st around; join with sl st in top of beg ch-2.
Rnds 6–13 Rep Rnds 4 and 5 four times.
Rnd 14 Rep Rnd 4.

Dec Rnd 15 Ch 1, turn, sc2tog around; join with sl st in first sc—20 sts.

Fasten off, leaving a long yarn tail. Thread tail into tapestry needle and through sts of last rnd. Pull to close opening at top of Hat.

Knot securely.

FINISHING

Weave in ends. •

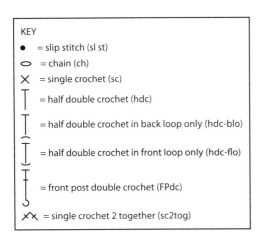

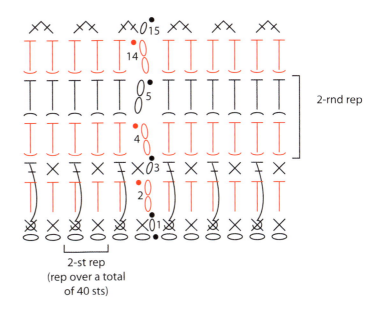

Hot Springs Hat and Scarf

Easy

MEASUREMENTS

HAT
Finished Circumference About 18"/45.5cm*
*Will stretch to fit a range of sizes.

SCARF
About 7 x 60"/18 x 152.5cm

MATERIALS

YARN
LION BRAND® Landscapes®, 3½oz/100g balls, each approx 147yd/134m (acrylic)
- 4 balls in #200 Tropics

HOOK
- One size K-10½ (6.5mm) crochet hook, *or size to obtain gauge*

NOTIONS
- Stitch markers
- Tapestry needle

GAUGE
12 sc = about 4"/10cm.
BE SURE TO CHECK YOUR GAUGE.

NOTES
1) Hat Rib is worked back and forth in rows, then sts are worked along one edge of rib and Hat is worked in the round.
2) Scarf Rib is worked same as Hat, then sts are worked along one edge to work length of Scarf.
3) A second rib section is worked and slip stitched to end of Scarf.

HAT

RIB
Ch 9.
Row 1 Sc in 2nd ch from hook and in each ch across—8 sc.
Row 2 Ch 1, turn, working in front loops only, sc in each st across.
Rep Row 2 until piece measures about 18"/45.5cm from beg, unstretched. Do not fasten off.

BODY
Rnd 1 (RS) Working across long side edge of ribbing, ch 1, work 56 sc evenly spaced across; join with sl st in first sc. Place marker for beg of rnd; move marker up as each rnd is completed.
Rnd 2 Ch 2 (counts as hdc), hdc in next st and in each st around.
Rnd 3 Hdc in each st around.
Rep Rnd 3 until piece measures about 8"/20.5cm from beg.

SHAPE CROWN
Rnd 1 *Sc in next 2 sts, sc2tog; rep from * around—you will have 42 sc.
Rnd 2 *Sc in next st, sc2tog; rep from * around—28 sc.
Rnd 3 Sc2tog around—14 sc.
Fasten off, leaving a long yarn tail. Thread tail through sts of Rnd 3 and pull to gather. Knot securely.

FINISHING
Sew short ends of Hat Rib tog. Weave in ends.

SCARF

BEGINNING RIB
Ch 16.

Row 1 Sc in 2nd ch from hook and in each ch across—15 sc.

Row 2 Ch 1, turn, working in front loops only, sc in each st across.

Rows 3–24 Rep Row 2.

SCARF
Row 1 (RS) Working across long side edge of rib, ch 1, work 22 sc evenly spaced across.

Row 2 Ch 2 (counts as first hdc), turn, hdc in next st and in each st across. Rep Row 2 until piece measures about 56"/142cm from beg. Fasten off.

ENDING RIB
Make same as Beginning Rib. With WS tog, sl st Ending Rib to last row of Scarf.

FINISHING
Weave in ends. •

Freshman Crocheted Hat

Beginner

MEASUREMENTS
Finished Circumference About 21"/53.5cm*
*Will stretch to fit a range of sizes.
Finished Height About 10½"/26.5cm

MATERIALS

YARN
LION BRAND® Homespun®, 6oz/170g balls, each approx 185yd/169m (acrylic/polyester) 5
- 1 ball in #368 Montana Sky

HOOK
- One size K-10½ (6.5mm) crochet hook, *or size to obtain gauge*

NOTION
- Tapestry needle

GAUGE
10 sc = about 4"/10cm.
BE SURE TO CHECK YOUR GAUGE.

NOTE
A flat rectangle is crocheted, then sewed together to make Hat.

HAT
Leaving a long yarn tail, ch 53.
Row 1 Sc in 2nd ch from hook and in each ch across —52 sc.
Row 2 Ch 1, turn. Sc in each st across.

Rep Row 2 until piece measures about 11"/28cm from beg. Fasten off, leaving a long yarn tail. Thread tail through sts of last row and pull to gather. Knot securely.

FINISHING
With beg yarn tail, sew sides of piece tog to make Hat. Weave in ends. ●

Simple Tweed Hat

Easy

MEASUREMENTS
Finished Circumference About 19"/48.5cm*
*Will stretch to fit a range of sizes.

MATERIALS
YARN
LION BRAND® Heartland®, 5oz/142g balls, each approx 251yd/230m (acrylic/rayon)
- 1 ball in #149 Great Smoky Mountains

HOOK
- One size K-10½ (6.5mm) crochet hook, *or size to obtain gauge*

NOTION
- Tapestry needle

GAUGE
11 sc = about 4"/10cm.
BE SURE TO CHECK YOUR GAUGE.

HAT
Ch 26.
Row 1 Sc in 2nd ch from hook and in each ch across —25 sc.
Row 2 Ch 1, turn. Working in back loops only, sc in each sc across.
Rep Row 2 until piece measures about 19"/48.5cm from beg. Fasten off, leaving a long yarn tail. Thread yarn tail through ends of rows along one long edge and pull to gather for top of Hat. Knot securely.

FINISHING
Seam short sides of piece to make Hat. Weave in ends. •

Phyllis Hat

Easy

MEASUREMENTS
Finished Circumference About 20"/51cm*
*Will stretch to fit a range of sizes.
Finished Height About 8"/20.5cm

MATERIALS
YARN
LION BRAND® Vanna's Choice®, 3½oz/100g balls, each approx 170yd/156m (acrylic) (4)
• 1 ball each in #109 Colonial Blue (A) and #105 Silver Blue (B)

HOOK
• One size J-10 (6mm) crochet hook, *or size to obtain gauge*

NOTIONS
• Tapestry needle

GAUGE
Rnds 1–4 = about 4"/10cm and 12 sc = about 4"/10cm in pattern.
BE SURE TO CHECK YOUR GAUGE.

STITCH GLOSSARY
beg-Cl (beg cluster) Yarn over, insert hook in indicated sp and draw up a loop, yarn over and draw through 2 loops on hook (2 loops on hook); yarn over, insert hook in same sp and draw up a loop, yarn over and draw through 2 loops on hook, yarn over and draw through all loops on hook.

Cl (cluster) Yarn over, insert hook in indicated sp and draw up a loop, yarn over and draw through 2 loops on hook, *yarn over, insert hook in same sp and draw up a loop, yarn over and draw through 2 loops on hook; rep from * once more, yarn over and draw through all loops on hook.

NOTES
1) Hat is worked in joined rnds beginning at the top.
2) Yarn color is changed at the end of rnds by working joining sl st with new color. Do not fasten off, carry unused color up wrong side of Hat until next needed. When carrying yarn don't pull it too tightly or let it hang too loosely.

HAT
With A, ch 4; join with sl st in first ch to form a ring.
Rnd 1 (RS) Ch 4 (counts as first dc, ch 1), [dc, ch 1] 7 times in ring; join with sl st in 3rd ch of beg ch—8 dc and 8 ch-1 sps.
Rnd 2 Ch 1, sl st in last ch-1 sp of Rnd 1, ch 3 (counts as first dc in this rnd and in all following rnds), 2 dc in same ch-1 sp, 3 dc in each ch-1 sp around; join with sl st in top of beg ch—24 dc (eight 3-dc groups).
Rnd 3 [Ch 3, 2 sc in sp between next two 3-dc groups] 8 times; join with sl st in first ch-3 sp—16 sc (eight 2-sc groups) and 8 ch-3 sps.
Rnd 4 Ch 3, 4 dc in same ch-3 sp, [ch 1, 5 dc in next ch-3 sp] 7 times, ch 1; join with sl st in top of beg ch—40 dc (eight 5-dc groups) and 8 ch-1 sps.
Rnd 5 Ch 1, working through back loops only, sc in same st as joining, sc in next 4 sts, ch 2, *sc in next 5 dc, ch 2; rep from * around; join with sl st in first sc—40 sc and 8 ch-2 sps.
Rnd 6 Sl st in next sc, ch 3, beg-Cl in same st, ch 2, sk next st, Cl in next st, *ch 2, Cl in next ch-2 sp, [ch 2, sk next st, Cl in next st] twice; rep from * to last ch-2 sp, Cl in last ch-2 sp, ch 2; join with sl st in top of beg Cl—24 clusters and 24 ch-2 sps.

Rnd 7 Sl st in next ch-2 sp, ch 3, 3 dc in same ch-2 sp, *ch 1, 4 dc in next ch-2 sp; rep from * around, ch 1; join with sl st in top of beg ch-3—96 dc (twenty-four 4-dc groups) and 24 ch-1 sps.

Rnd 8 *Ch 4, sk next 4 dc, 2 sc in next ch-1 sp; rep from * around; with B, join with sl st in first ch-4 sp—48 sc and 24 ch-4 sps.

Rnd 9 With B, ch 3, 2 dc in same ch-4 sp, 3 dc in each ch-4 sp around; with A, join with sl st in top of beg ch-3—72 dc (twenty-four 3-dc groups).

Rnd 10 With A, *ch 3, 2 sc in sp between next two 3-dc groups; rep from * around; join with sl st in first ch-3 sp—48 sc (twenty-four 2-sc groups) and 24 ch-3 sps.

Rnd 11 Ch 2 (counts as first hdc), 2 hdc in same ch-3 sp, [2 hdc in next ch-3 sp, 3 hdc in next ch-3 sp] 11 times, 2 hdc in last ch-3 sp; with B, join with sl st in top of beg ch—60 hdc (twelve 2-hdc groups and twelve 3-hdc groups).

Rnd 12 With B, *ch 2, 2 sc in sp between next 2 hdc groups; rep from * around; with A, join with sl st in first ch-2 sp—48 sc (twenty-four 2-sc groups) and 24 ch-2 sps.

Rnd 13 With A, ch 2 (counts as first hdc), 2 hdc in same ch-2 sp, [2 hdc in next ch-2 sp, 3 hdc in next ch-2 sp] 11 times, 2 hdc in last ch-2 sp; join with sl st in top of beg ch—60 hdc (twelve 2-hdc groups and twelve 3-hdc groups).

Rnd 14 With A, rep Rnd 12; join with B.

Rnd 15 With B, rep Rnd 13; join with A.

Rnd 16 With A, rep Rnd 12; join with B.

Rnds 17 and 18 With B, rep Rnds 13 and 14; join with A at end of Rnd 18.

Rnd 19 With A, rep Rnd 13; join with B.

Rnds 20 and 21 With B, rep Rnds 12 and 13; join with A at end of Rnd 21.

Rnd 22 With A, ch 1, sc in same sp, working through back loops only, sc in each st around; with B, join with sl st in first sc—60 sc. Fasten off A.

Rnd 23 With B, ch 1, working through back loops only, sc in each st around; join with sl st in first sc. Fasten off.

FINISHING

Weave in ends. •

Herringbone Hat

Easy

MEASUREMENTS
Finished Circumference About 19"/48.5cm*
*Will stretch to fit a range of sizes.

MATERIALS
YARN
LION BRAND® Wool-Ease®, 3oz/85g balls, each approx 197yd/180m (acrylic/wool) [4]
• 1 ball each in #151 Grey Heather (A) and #152 Oxford Grey (B)

HOOK
• One size H-8 (5mm) crochet hook, *or size to obtain gauge*

NOTIONS
• One pompom maker
• Tapestry needle
• 4 small buttons
• Sewing needle and thread

GAUGE
15 dc + 7 rnds = about 4"/10cm.
BE SURE TO CHECK YOUR GAUGE.

STITCH GLOSSARY
BPHDC (Back Post hdc) Yarn over, insert hook from back to front then to back again, going around post of indicated st, draw up a loop, yarn over and draw through all loops on hook. Skip st behind the BPHDC.

FPHDC (Front Post hdc) Yarn over, insert hook from front to back then to front, going around post of indicated st, draw up a loop, yarn over and draw through all loops on hook. Skip st behind the FPHDC.

FPDC (front post dc) Yarn over, insert hook from front to back then to front, going around post of indicated st, draw up a loop, (yarn over and draw through 2 loops on hook) twice. Skip st behind the FPDC.

NOTE
Hat is worked in one piece in the round with the right side always facing, beginning at top.

HAT
With A, ch 4; join with sl st to form a ring.
Rnd 1 Ch 2 (does not count as a st in this rnd and all following rnds), work 11 dc in ring; join with sl st in top of beg ch.
Rnd 2 Ch 2, (dc, FPDC) in each st around (first work dc, then work FPDC around same st); join with sl st in top of beg ch—you will have 22 sts.
Rnd 3 Ch 2, *(FPDC, dc) in next st (first work FPDC, then work dc behind it), (dc, FPDC) in next st (first work dc, then work FPDC around same st); rep from * around; join with sl st in top of beg ch—44 sts.
Rnd 4 Ch 2, *sk next FPDC, (FPDC, dc) in next dc, (dc, FPDC) in next dc, sk next FPDC; rep from * around; join with sl st in top of beg ch.
Rnd 5 Ch 2, *sk next FPDC, (FPDC, 2 dc) in next dc, (2 dc, FPDC) in next dc, sk next FPDC; rep from * around; join with sl st in top of beg ch—66 sts.
Rnd 6 Ch 2, *sk next FPDC, (FPDC, 2 dc) in next dc, dc in next 2 dc, (2 dc, FPDC) in next dc, sk next FPDC; rep from * around; join with sl st in top of beg ch—88 sts.
Rnd 7 Ch 2, *sk next FPDC, sk next dc, (FPDC, 2 dc) in next dc, dc in next 2 dc, (2 dc, FPDC) in next dc, sk next dc, sk next FPDC; rep from * around; join with sl st in top of beg ch—88 sts.
Rep Rnd 7 until Hat measures about 7½"/19cm from beg.

Dec Rnd Ch 2, *sk next FPDC, sk next dc, (FPDC, dc) in next dc, dc in next 2 dc, (dc, FPDC) in next dc, sk next dc, sk next FPDC; rep from * around; join with sl st in top of beg ch—66 sts.
Do NOT fasten off.

BAND

Rnd 1 Ch 1, *FPHDC in next FPDC, BPHDC in next dc, FPHDC in next 2 dc, BPHDC in next dc, FPHDC in next FPDC; rep from * around; join with sl st to beg ch—66 sts.

Rnd 2 Ch 1, *FPHDC, BPHDC, [FPHDC] twice, BPHDC, FPHDC; rep from * around; join with sl st to beg ch.

Rnds 3–10 Rep Rnd 2 for 7 more times. Fasten off.

FINISHING

Weave in ends.
With B, make a pompom. Tie pompom to top of Hat.
With sewing needle and thread, sew buttons to band. •

Shaded Stripes Hat

Easy

SIZE
Finished Circumference About 18"/46cm*
*Will stretch to fit a range of sizes.

MATERIALS
YARN
LION BRAND® Vanna's Choice®, 3½oz/100g balls, each approx 170yd/156m (acrylic) (4)
• 1 ball each in #108 Dusty Blue (A) and #118 Midnight Blue (B)

HOOKS
• One size I-9 (5.5mm) crochet hook, *or size to obtain gauge*
• One size G-6 (4mm) crochet hook

NOTION
• Tapestry needle

GAUGE
14 sts = about 4"/10cm in pattern using larger hook.
BE SURE TO CHECK YOUR GAUGE.

STITCH EXPLANATIONS
sc4tog (sc 4 sts tog) [Insert hook in next st and draw up a loop] 4 times, yarn over and draw through all 5 loops on hook—3 sts decreased.

NOTES
1) Hat Band is worked back and forth in rows, then ends are joined to make a ring. Body of Hat is worked in rounds beginning along one edge of seamed Band.
2) Yarn color is changed following a Stripe Sequence.
3) To change yarn color, work last st of old color to last yarn over. Yarn over with new color and draw through all loops to complete st. Carry unused color loosely along back of work until next needed.

STRIPE SEQUENCE
*Work 3 rnds with B, work 3 rnds with A; rep from * for Stripe Sequence.

HAT
BAND
With smaller hook and A, ch 10.
Row 1 Sc in 2nd ch from hook and in each ch across—9 sc.
Row 2 Ch 1, turn. Working through back loops only, sc in each st across.
Rep Row 2 until piece measures 18"/46cm from beg. Hold first and last rows tog, with sts matching.
Joining Row Ch 1, turn. Working through both thicknesses, sl st in each st across to join.
Do NOT fasten off.

BODY
Rnd 1 Continuing with A, and changing to larger hook, ch 1, work 80 sc evenly spaced around one long edge of Band; join with sl st in first sc—80 sc.
Rnd 2 Ch 1, sc in first st and in each st around; join with sl st in first sc—80 sc.

Beg Stripe Sequence
Note Beg on Rnd 3, work in Stripe Sequence. Continue in Stripe Sequence for rem of Hat.
Rnd 3 With B, sl st into each st around; join with sl st in first sl st.
Rnd 4 Ch 2 (does not count as first hdc in this rnd or in any of the following rnds), hdc in first st and in each st around; join with sl st in top of beg ch.

Rnd 5 Ch 2, hdc in first 2 sts, *hdc2tog, hdc in the next 6 sts; rep from * to last 6 sts, hdc2tog, hdc in next 4 sts; join with sl st in top of beg ch—70 hdc at end of this rnd.
Rnd 6 Rep Rnd 3.
Rnds 7 and 8 Rep Rnd 4.
Rnds 9–11 Rep Rnds 6–8.
Rnds 12 and 13 Rep Rnds 3 and 4.
Rnd 14 Ch 2, hdc in first 5 sts, *hdc2tog, hdc in next 5 sts; rep from * to last 2 sts, hdc2tog; join with sl st in top of beg ch—60 hdc.
Rnds 15–17 Rep Rnds 6–8.
Rnds 18 and 19 Rep Rnds 3 and 4.
Rnd 20 Ch 2, hdc in first st, hdc2tog, *hdc in next 4 sts, hdc2tog; rep from * to last 3 sts, hdc in last 3 sts; join with sl st in top of beg ch—50 hdc.

Rnds 21–23 Rep Rnds 6–8.
Rnds 24 and 25 Ch 1, sc in first st and in each st around; join with sl st in first sc.
Rnd 26 Ch 1, sc in first st, sc4tog, *sc in next st, sc4tog; rep from * around; join with sl st in first sc—20 sc.
Rnd 27 With A, ch 1, sc4tog around; join with sl st in first sc—5 sc.
Fasten off, leaving a long yarn tail. Thread tail through sts of last rnd and pull to gather. Knot securely.

FINISHING

Weave in ends. •

Sophomore Crochet Hat

Easy

MEASUREMENTS
Finished Circumference About 20½"/52cm*
*Will stretch to fit a range of sizes.
Finished Height About 10"/25.5cm

MATERIALS
YARN
LION BRAND® Vanna's Choice®, 3½oz/100g balls, each approx 170yd/156m (acrylic)
- 1 ball in #135 Rust

HOOK
- One size J-10 (6mm) crochet hook, *or size to obtain gauge*

NOTION
- Tapestry needle

GAUGE
14 hdc = about 4"/10cm.
BE SURE TO CHECK YOUR GAUGE.

NOTES
1) Hat is worked in joined rnds.
2) Long ending yarn tail is woven through sts of last rnd to gather top of Hat.
3) If you find it difficult to join the beg ch into a ring without twisting the ch, Rnd 1 can be worked as a row, then joined into a rnd, as follows: Leaving a long beg tail, ch 72, hdc in 3rd ch from hook (2 skipped ch count as first hdc) and in each ch across; join with sl st in top of beg ch—71 hdc. Use beg tail to sew gap at base of first row closed. Proceed to Rnd 2.

HAT
Ch 71. Taking care not to twist ch, join with sl st in first ch to form a ring.
Rnd 1 Ch 2 (counts as first hdc in this rnd and in all following rnds), hdc in next ch and in each ch around; join with sl st in top of beg ch—71 hdc.
Rnd 2 Ch 2, hdc in each hdc around; join with sl st in top of beg ch.
Rep Rnd 2 until piece measures about 10"/25.5cm from beg.
Fasten off, leaving a long tail. Thread tail through sts of last rnd and pull to gather. Knot securely.

FINISHING
Weave in ends. •

Shaded Hat and Wristers

Easy

MEAUREMENTS

HAT
Finished Circumference About 19"/48.5cm*
*Will stretch to fit a range of sizes.

WRISTERS
Finished Circumference About 8"/20.5cm
Finished Length About 6½"/16.5cm

MATERIALS

YARN
LION BRAND® Landscapes®, 3½oz/100g balls, each approx 147yd/134m (acrylic)
- 2 balls in #202 Mountain Range

HOOKS
- One size K-10½ (6.5mm) crochet hook, *or size to obtain gauge*
- One size I-9 (5.5mm) crochet hook

TAPESTRY
- Tapestry needle

GAUGE
12 hdc = about 4"/10cm with larger hook.
BE SURE TO CHECK YOUR GAUGE.

NOTES
1) The Hat and Wristers are in an easy pattern that uses increases and decreases to create diagonal color shading.
2) The first section of Hat and Wristers is shaped with increases and the last section is shaped with decreases. In the center section, an increase is worked at one end and a decrease is worked at the other end of each row, so the stitch count will not change.

HAT
With larger hook, ch 3.

INCREASE SECTION
Row 1 Work 2 hdc in 3rd ch from hook (2 skipped ch do not count as a st)—you will have 2 hdc in this row.
Row 2 Ch 2 (does not count as a st throughout), turn, 2 hdc in each st—4 hdc.
Rows 3–15 Ch 2, turn, 2 hdc in first st, hdc in each st to last st, 2 hdc in last st—30 hdc at end of Row 15.

CENTER SECTION
Row 1 Ch 2, turn, hdc2tog, hdc in each st to last st, 2 hdc in last st.

Shaded Hat and Wristers

Row 2 Ch 2 (does not count as a st throughout), turn, 2 hdc in first st, hdc in each st to last 2 sts, hdc2tog. Rep Rows 1 and 2 until longest straight edge measures about 19"/48.5cm.

DECREASE SECTION

Rows 1–13 Ch 2 (does not count as a st throughout), turn, hdc2tog, hdc in each st to last 2 sts, hdc2tog—4 hdc at end of Row 13.
Row 14 Ch 2, turn, [hdc2tog] twice—2 hdc.
Row 15 Ch 2, turn, hdc2tog—1 hdc.
Fasten off, leaving a long yarn tail for sewing.
Thread yarn tail into blunt and sew sides of Hat tog.

BAND

Note Band is worked back and forth in rows and is joined to Hat at end of every other row.
From RS, with smaller hook, working around one open end of Hat, join yarn with a sl st in end of first row following Hat seam.
Set-up Rnd Ch 1, work an even number of sc evenly spaced around edge of Hat; join with sl st in first sc.
Row 1 Ch 8, sc in 2nd ch from hook and in each ch across; sl st into next sc on edge of Hat—7 sc.
Row 2 Sl st into next sc on edge of Hat, turn, working in back loops only, sc in each st across.
Row 3 Ch 1, turn, working in back loops only, sc in each st across; sl st into next sc on edge of Hat.
Rep Rows 2 and 3 until band has been worked all around edge of Hat, end with a Row 2 as last row you work.
Fasten off, leaving a long yarn tail for sewing. Thread yarn tail into tapestry needle and sew ends of band tog.

FINISHING

Thread tapestry needle with a doubled strand of yarn. Weave needle in and out through spaces at ends of rows around end of Hat opposite band. Pull ends of strand to close top of Hat and knot. From wrong side, sew any openings at top of Hat closed.
Weave in ends.

WRISTERS (MAKE 2)

With larger hook, ch 3.

INCREASE SECTION

Row 1 Work 2 hdc in 3rd ch from hook (2 skipped ch do not count as a st)—you will have 2 hdc in this row.
Row 2 Ch 2 (does not count as a st throughout), turn, 2 hdc in each st—4 hdc.
Rows 3–9 Ch 2, turn. 2 hdc in first st, hdc in each st to last st, 2 hdc in last st—18 hdc at end of Row 9.

CENTER SECTION

Row 1 Ch 2 (does not count as a st throughout), turn, hdc2tog, hdc in each st to last st, 2 hdc in last st.
Row 2 Ch 2, turn, 2 hdc in first st, hdc in each st to last 2 sts, hdc2tog.
Rep Rows 1 and 2 until longest straight edge measures about 8"/20.5cm.

DECREASE SECTION

Rows 1–7 Ch 2 (does not count as a st throughout), turn, hdc2tog, hdc in each st to last 2 sts, hdc2tog—4 hdc at the end of Row 7.
Row 8 Ch 2, turn, [hdc2tog] twice—2 hdc.
Row 9 Ch 2, turn, hdc2tog—1 hdc.
Fasten off, leaving a long yarn tail for sewing. Sew short ends of piece tog, leaving an opening for thumb.

CUFF

Note Cuff is worked back and forth in rows and is joined to wrist edge at end of every other row.
From RS, with smaller hook, join yarn with a sl st in end of first row following seam.
Set-up Rnd Ch 1, work an even number of sc evenly spaced around edge of Wrister; join with sl st in first sc.
Row 1 Ch 8, sc in 2nd ch from hook and in each ch across; sl st into next sc on edge of Wrister—7 sc.
Rows 2 and 3 Working around edge of Wrister, work as for Rows 2 and 3 of Hat band.

Rep Rows 2 and 3 until Cuff has been worked all around edge of Wrister, end with a Row 2 as last row you work. Fasten off, leaving a long yarn tail for sewing. Use yarn tail to sew ends of cuff tog.

FINISHING
Weave in ends. •

Textured Hat

Easy

MEAUREMENTS
Finished Circumference About 21"/53.5cm*

*Will stretch to fit a range of sizes.

MATERIALS
YARN
LION BRAND® Wool-Ease® Thick & Quick®, 6oz/170g balls, each approx 106yd/97m (acrylic/wool)
- 1 ball in #154 Grey Marble

HOOK
- One size P-15 (10mm) crochet hook, *or size to obtain gauge*

NOTIONS
- Tapestry needle

GAUGE
2 (sc, 2 dc) groups = about 3½"/9cm.
BE SURE TO CHECK YOUR GAUGE.

NOTES
1) Hat is made from a rectangle worked back and forth in rows in an easy stitch pattern.
2) Short ends of rectangle are sewn together to make Hat.

HAT
Ch 39.

Row 1 Work 2 dc in 3rd ch from hook (2 skipped ch count as beg ch), *sk next 2 ch, (sc, 2 dc) in next ch; rep from * 10 more times, sk next 2 ch, sc in last ch—you will have 36 sts in this row, consisting of 11 (sc, 2 dc) groups, 2 dc at beg of row and 1 sc at end of row. **Note** 2 dc at beg and sc at end count as 1 more (sc, 2 dc) group.

Row 2 Ch 2 (does not count as a st), turn. 2 dc in first sc, *sk next 2 dc, (sc, 2 dc) in next sc; rep from * 10 more times, sk next 2 dc, sc in top of beg ch.
Rep Row 2 until piece measures about 11"/28cm from beg.
Fasten off, leaving a long yarn tail.

FINISHING
Thread yarn tail into tapestry needle and sew short ends of piece tog to make a tube. Weave tail in and out through sts around one end of tube and pull to gather for top of Hat. Knot securely.
Weave in ends. •

Saratoga Hat

Easy

MEASUREMENTS
Finished Circumference About 18"/45.5cm*
*Will stretch to fit a range of sizes.

MATERIALS
YARN
LION BRAND® Landscapes®, 3½oz/100g balls, each approx 147yd/134m (acrylic) 4
- 1 ball in #215 Fiesta

HOOK
- One size K-10½ (6.5mm) crochet hook, *or size to obtain gauge*

NOTIONS
- Stitch markers
- Tapestry needle

GAUGE
12 sc = about 4"/10cm.
BE SURE TO CHECK YOUR GAUGE.

NOTE
Ribbed band is worked back and forth in rows, then sts for Hat are picked up along band and worked in rnds.

HAT
RIBBED BAND
Ch 9.
Row 1 Sc in 2nd ch from hook and each ch across—8 sc.
Row 2 Ch 1, turn, working in front loops only, sc in each st across.
Rep Row 2 until piece measures about 18"/45.5cm from beg, unstretched. Do not fasten off.

BODY
Rnd 1 (RS) Working across one long side edge of ribbing, ch 1, work 56 sc evenly spaced across; join with sl st in first sc.
Place marker for beg of rnd; move marker up as each rnd is completed.
Rnd 2 Ch 2 (counts as hdc), hdc in next st and each st around.
Rnd 3 Hdc in each st around.
Rep Rnd 3 until piece measures about 8"/20.5cm from beg.

SHAPE CROWN
Rnd 1 *Sc in next 2 sts, sc2tog; rep from * around—you will have 42 sc.
Rnd 2 *Sc in next st, sc2tog; rep from * around—28 sc.
Rnd 3 Sc2tog around—14 sc.
Fasten off, leaving a long yarn tail.
Thread tail into tapestry needle, draw through sts of Rnd 3 and pull to gather. Knot securely.

FINISHING
Sew short ends of ribbed band tog. Weave in ends. •

Next Generation Hat and Scarf

Easy

SIZES
Child's S (M, L)

MEASUREMENTS
HAT
Finished Circumference About 15 (17, 19)"/38 (43, 48.5)cm*
*Will stretch to fit a range of sizes.
Finished Height About 6½ (6½, 7½)"/16 (16, 19)cm
SCARF
About 6 x 40"/15 x 101cm

MATERIALS
YARN
LION BRAND® Heartland®, 5oz/142g balls, each approx 251yd/230m (acrylic/rayon)
• 1 ball each in #398 Acadia Tweed (A) and #389 Isle Royale Tweed (B)

HOOK
• One size H-8 (5mm) crochet hook, *or size to obtain gauge*

NOTIONS
• Tapestry needle

GAUGE
14 hdc = about 4"/10cm.
BE SURE TO CHECK YOUR GAUGE.

NOTES
1) Scarf and hat are each worked in one piece, changing color to create stripes.
2) To change color, work last st of old color to last yarn over. Yarn over with new color and draw through all loops to complete st. For wide stripes, fasten off old color and proceed with new color. For narrow stripes, carry color not in use up side of piece.

HAT
With B, ch 54, (60, 64). Join with sl st in first ch to form a ring, being careful not to twist sts.
Rnd 1 Ch 2 (counts as first hdc in this rnd and in all following rnds), hdc in next ch and in each ch around; join with sl st in top of beg ch—54 (60, 64) sts.
Rnd 2 Ch 2, hdc in next hdc and in each hdc around; join with sl st in top of beg ch.
Rep Rnd 2 as follows: Work 5 (5, 6) rnds with A, 5 (5, 6) rnds with B. Fasten off B. Work 2 rnds with A only.

SHAPE CROWN
Dec Rnd 1 Ch 2, hdc in next 3 sts, hdc2tog, *hdc in next 4 sts, hdc2tog; rep from * around; join with sl st in top of beg ch—you will have 45 (50, 55) hdc at end of this rnd.
Dec Rnd 2 Ch 2, hdc in next 2 sts, hdc2tog, *hdc in next 3 sts, hdc2tog; rep from * around; join with sl st in top of beg ch—36 (40, 44) hdc.
Dec Rnd 3 Ch 2, hdc in next st, hdc2tog, *hdc in next 2 sts, hdc2tog; rep from * around; join with sl st in top of beg ch—27 (30, 33) hdc.
Dec Rnd 4 Ch 2, hdc2tog, *hdc in next st, hdc2tog; rep from * around; join with sl st in top of beg ch—18 (20, 22) hdc.
Dec Rnd 5 Ch 1, hdc in next st (beg ch and hdc count as first hdc2tog), *hdc2tog; rep from * around; join with sl st in first hdc—9 (10, 11) hdc.
Fasten off, leaving a long yarn tail. Thread yarn tail through rem sts and pull to gather. Knot securely.

FINISHING
Weave in ends.

SCARF

With A, ch 22.

Row 1 Hdc in 3rd ch from hook (beg ch counts as first hdc) and in each ch across—21 hdc.

Row 2 Ch 2 (counts as first hdc), turn, hdc in next hdc and in each hdc across.

Rep Row 2 as follows:

Work 3 more rows with A, 3 rows with B, 41 rows with A, 41 rows with B, 3 rows with A, 5 rows with B.

Fasten off.

FINISHING

Weave in ends. •

Woven Beanie

Easy

MEASUREMENTS
Finished Circumference About 18"/45.5cm*
*Will stretch to fit a range of sizes.
Finished Height About 9"/23cm

MATERIALS
YARN
LION BRAND® Scarfie®, 5.3oz/150g balls, each approx 312yd/285m (acrylic/wool)
- 1 ball in #234 Steel Blue/Slate

HOOK
- One size K-10½ (6.5mm) crochet hook, *or size to obtain gauge*

NOTION
- Tapestry needle

GAUGE
15 sts + 11 rnds = about 4½"/11.5cm in Basketweave pattern of Rnds 7–12.
BE SURE TO CHECK YOUR GAUGE.

STITCH GLOSSARY
BPdc (Back Post dc) Yarn over, insert hook from back to front then to back, going around post of indicated st, draw up a loop, [yarn over and draw through 2 loops on hook] twice. Sk top of st in front of BPdc.

FPdc (Front Post dc) Yarn over, insert hook from front to back then to front, going around post of indicated st, draw up a loop, [yarn over and draw through 2 loops on hook] twice. Sk top of st behind FPdc.

NOTES
1) Beanie is worked from the lower edge upwards.
2) A ribbed band is worked back and forth in rows, then short ends are joined to make a circle.
3) Stitches are worked along one edge of circle, then Beanie is worked upwards in joined rnds in Basketweave pattern.

BEANIE
LOWER BAND
Ch 9.
Row 1 (RS) Sc in 2nd ch from hook and in each ch across—you will have 8 sc in this row.
Row 2–60 Ch 1, turn, working in back loops only, sc in each st across.
Bring short ends of piece tog, matching sts.
Joining Row From WS, and working through both thicknesses, sl st in each st across to join piece into a circle. Turn band RS out. Do NOT fasten off.

BODY
Note When joining last st of each rnd to top of beg ch, insert hook from back to front under loops at top of beg ch, yarn over and draw through all loops on hook to complete join.

Rnd 1 (RS) Ch 2 (does not count as a st), working along edge of band, dc in end of each row around; join with sl st in top of beg ch-2—60 dc.

Basketweave Pattern
Rnds 2–3 Ch 2 (counts as first FPdc), FPdc around each of next 2 sts, *BPdc around each of next 3 sts, FPdc around each of next 3 sts; rep from * to last 3 sts, BPdc around each of last 3 sts; join with sl st in top of beg ch-2.

Rnds 4–6 Ch 2 (counts as first BPdc), BPdc around each of next 2 sts, *FPdc around each of next 3 sts, BPdc around each of next 3 sts; rep from * to last 3 sts, FPdc around each of last 3 sts; join with sl st in top of beg ch-2.

Rnds 7–9 Rep Rnd 2 for 3 times.

Rnds 10–12 Rep Rnds 4–6.

Rnds 13–18 Rep Rnds 7–12.

Fasten off, leaving a long yarn tail. Thread tail into tapestry needle, then through top of sts of last rnd. Pull to close opening at top of Beanie and knot.

FINISHING

Weave in ends. •

Heige Hat

Easy

MEASUREMENTS
Finished Circumference About 20"/51cm*
*Will stretch to fit a range of sizes.
Finished Height About 8"/20.5cm

MATERIALS
YARN
LION BRAND® Scarfie®, 5.3oz/150g balls, each approx 312yd/285m (acrylic/wool) 5
- 1 ball in #206 Cream/Taupe

HOOK
- One size K-10½ (6.5mm) crochet hook, *or size to obtain gauge*

NOTIONS
- Tapestry needle

GAUGE
11 hdc = about 4"/10cm.
BE SURE TO CHECK YOUR GAUGE.

STITCH GLOSSARY
Bobble Yarn over, insert hook in indicated st and draw up a loop, yarn over and draw through 2 loops on hook (2 loops rem on hook), [yarn over, insert hook in same st and draw up a loop, yarn over and draw through 2 loops on hook] 3 times (5 loops rem on hook), yarn over, draw through all loops on hook.

NOTES
1) Hat is worked in one piece in joined rnds, beginning at top of Hat.
2) All rnds in Bobble band are worked on WS. This becomes the RS when the band is folded up.

HAT
Ch 3.

Rnd 1 (RS) Work 8 hdc in 3rd ch from hook (2 skipped ch do not count as a st), join with sl st in first hdc—you will have 8 hdc.

Rnd 2 Ch 2 (does not count as a st), 2 hdc in each st around; join with sl st in first hdc—you will have 16 hdc at end of this rnd.

Rnd 3 Ch 2 (does not count as a st), hdc in first st, 2 hdc in next st, *hdc in next st, 2 hdc in next st; rep from * around; join with sl st in first hdc—24 hdc.

Rnd 4 Ch 2 (does not count as a st), hdc in first 2 sts, 2 hdc in next st, *hdc in next 2 sts, 2 hdc in next st; rep from * around; join with sl st in first hdc—32 hdc.

Rnd 5 Ch 2 (does not count as a st), hdc in first 3 sts, 2 hdc in next st, *hdc in next 3 sts, 2 hdc in next st; rep from * around; join with sl st in first hdc—40 hdc.

Rnd 6 Ch 2 (does not count as a st), hdc in first 4 sts, 2 hdc in next st, *hdc in next 4 sts, 2 hdc in next st; rep from * around; join with sl st in first hdc—48 hdc.

Rnd 7 Ch 2 (does not count as a st), hdc in first 5 sts, 2 hdc in next st, *hdc in next 5 sts, 2 hdc in next st; rep from * around; join with sl st in first hdc—56 hdc.

Rnds 8–19 Ch 2 (does not count as a st), hdc in each st around; join with sl st in first hdc.

BOBBLE BAND
Note When you turn your work at beg of Set-up Rnd, you will be working on WS. Continue to work only on WS (NOT turning) until all rnds of Bobble Band are complete. This becomes RS when band is folded up.

Set-up Rnd (WS) Ch 1, turn, working in back loops only, sc in each st around; join with sl st in beg ch-1—56 sc.

Rnd 1 Ch 3 (does not count as a st), do NOT turn, *Bobble in next st, dc in next st; rep from * around; join with sl st in top of beg ch-3—28 Bobbles and 28 dc.

Rnd 2 Ch 1, sc in each st around; join with sl st in beg ch-1—56 sc.

Rnd 3 Ch 3 (does not count as a st), *dc in next st, Bobble in next st; rep from * around; join with sl st in top of beg ch-3.

Rnd 4 Rep Rnd 2.

Rnds 5 and 6 Rep Rnds 1 and 2.

Fasten off.

FINISHING

Weave in ends. •

Two Color Slouch Hat

Easy

MEASUREMENTS
Finished Circumference About 21"/53.5cm*
*Will stretch to fit a range of sizes.
Finished Height About 12"/30.5cm

MATERIALS
YARN
LION BRAND® Vanna's Choice®, 3½oz/100g balls, each approx 170yd/156m (acrylic)
• 1 ball each in #118 Midnight Blue (A) and #150 Pale Grey (B)

HOOK
• One size I-9 (5.5mm) crochet hook, *or size to obtain gauge*

NOTIONS
• Stitch markers
• Tapestry needle

GAUGE
13 sts = about 4"/10cm over Rnds 1–5.
Note Each sc and ch-1 sp count as 1 st.
BE SURE TO CHECK YOUR GAUGE.

NOTES
1) Hat is worked in one piece, in joined and turned rnds.
2) Yarn quantities are sufficient to make a second Hat, just reverse the colors.
3) If you find it difficult to join the beg ch into a ring without twisting the ch, Rnd 1 can be worked as a row, then joined into a rnd, as follows: Leaving a long beg tail, ch 71, sc in 2nd ch from hook, *ch 1, sk next ch, sc in next ch; rep from * to last ch, ch 1, sk last ch; join with sl st in first sc—you will have 35 sc and 35 ch-1 sps at the end of this row/rnd. Use beg tail to sew gap at base of first row closed. Proceed to Rnd 2.
4) Lower band of Hat is worked using both yarn colors. Body of Hat is worked with one color of yarn.
5) When working lower band, the yarn color is changed every other rnd. To change color, remove loop of old color from hook and elongate loop so that it does not unravel. Do not fasten off old color until instructed. Join new color as instructed or return elongated loop of new color to hook and gently tighten loop around hook. Proceed with new color. This color change method reduces the number of yarn tails you'll need to weave in later.

HAT
Beg at lower edge with A, ch 70; taking care not to twist ch, join with sl st in first ch to form a ring.
Rnd 1 (RS) With A, ch 1, sc in same ch as joining, *ch 1, sk next ch, sc in next ch; rep from * to last ch, ch 1, sk last ch; join with sl st in first sc—you will have 35 sc and 35 ch-1 sps in this rnd.

TWO COLOR LOWER BAND
Rnd 2 (WS) With A, ch 1, turn, sc in first ch-1 sp, *ch 1, sk next sc, sc in next ch-1 sp; rep from * to last sc, ch 1, sk last sc; join with sl st in first sc. Remove loop of A from hook. Elongate loop or place it on a stitch marker or safety pin so that it does not unravel.
Rnd 3 (RS) From RS, join B with sc in any ch-1 sp, *ch 1, sk next sc, sc in next ch-1 sp; rep from * to last sc, ch 1, sk last sc; join with sl st in first sc. Remove loop of B from hook. Elongate loop or place it on a stitch marker so it does not unravel. Return loop of A to hook and gently tighten loop around hook.
Rnd 4 (WS) With A, rep Rnd 2. Remove loop of A from hook. Elongate loop or place it on a stitch marker so it does not unravel. Return loop of B to hook and gently

tighten loop around hook.

Rnd 5 (RS) With B, rep Rnd 2. Remove loop of B from hook. Elongate loop or place it on a stitch marker so it does not unravel. Return loop of A to hook and gently tighten loop around hook.

Rnds 6 and 7 Rep Rnds 4 and 5. At end of Rnd 7, fasten off B. Return loop of A to hook and gently tighten loop around hook.

BODY

Rnds 8–38 With A, rep Rnd 2.

Rnd 39 With A, ch 1, turn, sc in first ch-1 sp, *sk next sc, sc in next ch-1 sp; rep from * to last sc, sk last sc; join with sl st in first sc—35 sc.

Fasten off, leaving a long yarn tail. Thread tail through top of sts of last rnd. Pull tail to close opening at top of Hat. Knot securely.

FINISHING

Weave in ends. •

Junior Crocheted Hat

Easy

MEASUREMENTS
Finished Circumference About 18"/45.5cm*
*Hat will stretch to fit a range of sizes.
Finished Length About 10"/25.5cm

MATERIALS
YARN
LION BRAND® Vanna's Choice®, 3½oz/100g balls, each approx 170yd/156m (acrylic)
- 1 ball each in #109 Colonial Blue (A) and #172 Kelly Green (B)

HOOK
- One size K-10½ (6.5mm) crochet hook, *or size to obtain gauge*

NOTION
- Tapestry needle

GAUGE
12 hdc = about 4"/10cm.
BE SURE TO CHECK YOUR GAUGE.

NOTES
1) Hat is worked in one piece, changing yarn color to create stripes, and then seamed.
2) To change color, work last stitch of old color to the last yarn over. Yarn over with new color and draw through all loops on hook to complete the stitch. Carry old color along the wrong side of the Hat.

HAT
With A, and leaving a long yarn tail, ch 56.
Row 1 Hdc in 3rd ch from hook and in each ch across —at end of Row 1 you will have 54 hdc.

Row 2 Ch 2, turn, hdc in each st across, changing to B in last st.
Rep Row 2, working 2 rows each with A and B alternately until piece measures about 9½"/24cm from beg, and ending with a 2nd row of B.
Change to A.
Next Row With A, ch 2, turn, *hdc in each of next 4 sts, hdc2tog; rep from * across—45 hdc.
Next Row With A, ch 2, turn, *hdc in each of next 3 sts, hdc2tog; rep from * across—36 hdc.
Fasten off, leaving a long yarn tail. Thread tail through sts of last rnd and pull to gather. Knot securely.

FINISHING
Seam sides of piece to make Hat.
Weave in ends. •

Pennington Hat

Easy

MEASUREMENTS
Finished Circumference About 19"/48.5cm*
*Will stretch to fit a range of sizes.
Finished Height About 12"/30.5cm

MATERIALS
YARN
LION BRAND® Mandala®, 5.3oz/150g balls, each approx 590yd/540m (acrylic)
- 2 balls in #211 Pocket Watch

HOOK
- One size N (10mm) crochet hook, *or size to obtain gauge*

NOTIONS
- Tapestry needle
- Extra-large pompom maker

GAUGE
8 sc = about 4"/10cm.
BE SURE TO CHECK YOUR GAUGE.

HAT
Chain 25.
Row 1 Sc in 2nd chain from hook and in each ch across—24 sc.
Row 2 Ch 1, turn, working in back loops only, sc in each sc across.
Rep Row 2 until piece measures about 19"/48.5cm from beg.
Fasten off, leaving a long yarn tail. Thread tail into tapestry needle and weave through ends of rows along one long edge and pull to gather for top of Hat. Knot securely.

FINISHING
Seam ends to make Hat.
Following package directions, make a pompom.
Tie pompom to top of Hat.
Weave in ends. •

Wave Pattern Hat and Cowl

Easy

MEASUREMENTS

HAT
Finished Circumference About 20"/51cm*
*Will stretch to fit a range of sizes.
Finished Height About 8½"/21.5cm

COWL
Finished Circumference About 33"/84cm
Finished Height About 12"/30.5cm

MATERIALS

YARN
LION BRAND® Heartland®, 5oz/142g balls, each approx 251yd/230m (acrylic/rayon)
- 2 balls* in #350 Mount Rainier Tweed

*You'll need one ball of yarn to make the Hat only, 2 balls to make the Cowl only.

HOOK
- One size J-10 (6mm) crochet hook, *or size to obtain gauge*

NOTION
- Tapestry needle

GAUGE
1 wave + 5 rows/rnds = about 4"/10cm.
BE SURE TO CHECK YOUR GAUGE.

STITCH GLOSSARY

dc4tog (dc 4 sts tog) [Yarn over, insert hook in next st and draw up a loop, yarn over and draw through 2 loops] 4 times, yarn over and draw through all 5 loops on hook—3 sts decreased.

NOTES

1) Cowl is worked back and forth in rows. The piece is twisted, then ends are sewn together to make a Mobius ring.

2) Hat is worked in joined and turned rnds beg at lower edge.

HAT

Ch 60. Taking care not to twist ch, join with sl st in first ch to form a ring.

Rnd 1 Ch 3 (does not count as a st in this rnd or in any rnd in this pattern), sk first ch, dc in next ch, dc2tog, *2 dc in each of next 4 ch, [dc2tog] 4 times; rep from * to last 8 ch, 2 dc in each of next 4 ch, [dc2tog] twice; join with sl st in top of beg ch—5 "waves" (60 dc).

Rnds 2–7 Ch 3, turn, sk first st, dc in next st, dc2tog, *2 dc in each of next 4 sts, [dc2tog] 4 times; rep from * to last 8 sts, 2 dc in each of next 4 sts, [dc2tog] twice; join with sl st in top of beg ch.

SHAPE CROWN

Rnd 8 Ch 3, turn, sk first st, dc in next st, *dc2tog, dc in next st, 2 dc in each of next 2 sts, dc in next st, dc2tog, dc4tog; rep from * to last 10 sts, dc2tog, dc in next st, 2 dc in each of next 2 sts, dc in next st, [dc2tog] twice; join with sl st in top of beg ch—45 dc.

Rnd 9 Ch 3, turn, sk first st, dc in next st, dc in next 3 sts, *[dc2tog] 3 times, dc in next 3 sts; rep from * to last 4 sts, [dc2tog] twice; join with sl st in top of beg ch—30 dc.

Rnd 10 Ch 3, turn, sk first st, dc in next st, *dc2tog; rep from * around; join with sl st in top of beg ch—15 dc.

Rnd 11 Ch 3, turn, sk first st, *dc2tog; rep from * around; join with sl st in top of beg ch—7 dc.

Rnd 12 Ch 1, turn, sc in each st around; join with sl st in first sc.

Fasten off, leaving a long yarn tail. Thread tail through remaining sts and pull to gather. Knot securely.

FINISHING
Weave in ends.

COWL
Ch 38.

Row 1 Dc in 4th ch from hook (beg ch does not count as a st), dc2tog, *2 dc in each of next 4 ch, [dc2tog] 4 times; rep from * to last 8 ch, 2 dc in each of next 4 ch, [dc2tog] twice—3 "waves" (36 dc).

Row 2 Ch 3 (does not count as a st), turn, sk first st, dc in next st, dc2tog, *2 dc in each of next 4 sts, [dc2tog] 4 times; rep from * to last 8 sts, 2 dc in each of next 4 sts, [dc2tog] twice.

Rep Row 2 until piece measures about 33"/84cm from beg. Fasten off.

FINISHING
Lay piece flat. Turn one of the ends over (180 degree turn) to put a twist in the piece. Keeping the twist, sew the short ends tog.

Weave in ends. •

The Casual Friday Hat

Easy

MEASUREMENTS
Finished Circumference About 20"/51cm*
*Will stretch to fit a range of sizes.
Finished Height About 11½"/29cm

MATERIALS
YARN
LION BRAND® Heartland®, 5oz/142g balls, each approx 251yd/230m (acrylic/rayon) (4)
• 1 ball each in #109 Olympic (A) and #158 Yellowstone (B)

HOOK
• One size I-9 (5.5mm) crochet hook, *or size to obtain gauge*

NOTION
• Tapestry needle

GAUGE
13 sc + 17 rnds = about 4"/10cm.
BE SURE TO CHECK YOUR GAUGE.

NOTES
1) Hat is worked in joined and turned rnds, beg at lower edge.
2) To change color, work last st with old color to last yarn over. Yarn over with new color and draw through all loops on hook to complete st. Proceed with new color. Fasten off old color.
3) If you find it difficult to join the beg ch into a ring without twisting the ch, Rnd 1 can be worked as a row, then joined into a rnd, as follows: Leaving a long beg tail, ch 65, sc in 2nd ch from hook and in each ch across; join with sl st in first sc—64 sc. Use beg tail to sew gap at base of first row closed. Proceed to Rnd 2.

HAT
BRIM
With B, ch 64, taking care not to twist ch, join with sl st in first ch to form ring.
Rnd 1 (RS) Ch 1, sc in same ch as joining, sc in each ch around, join with sl st in first sc—64 sts.
Rnds 2–5 Ch 1, turn, sc in each st around, join with sl st in first sc. Change to A in last st.

BODY
Rnd 6 With A, ch 1, turn, sc in each st around, join with sl st in first sc.
Rep Rnd 6 until piece measures about 10"/25.5cm from beg; end with a WS rnd. **Note** End with a WS rnd means that the last rnd you work should be a WS rnd, and the next rnd that you are ready to work will be a RS rnd.

SHAPE CROWN
Rnd 1 (RS) Ch 1, turn, *sc in next 3 sts, sc2tog, sc in next 3 sts; rep from * around, join with sl st in first sc—56 sts.
Rnd 2 Ch 1, turn, sc in each st around, join with sl st in first sc.
Rnd 3 Ch 1, turn, *sc in next st, sc2tog, sc in next st; rep from * around, join with sl st in first sc—42 sts.
Rnd 4 Ch 1, turn, sc in each st around, join with sl st in first sc.
Rnd 5 Ch 1, turn, *sc2tog; rep from * around, join with sl st in first sc—21 sts.
Fasten off, leaving a long yarn tail for sewing. Use yarn tail to sew top of Hat closed.

POCKET
With B, ch 10.
Row 1 Sc in 2nd ch from hook and in each ch across, change to A in last st—9 sts.
Rows 2–7 With A, ch 1, turn, sc in each st across.

Rows 8–10 Ch 1, turn, sc2tog, sc in each st to last 2 sts, sc2tog—3 sts at end of Row 10.

Row 11 Ch 1, turn, sc3tog. Fasten off.

FINISHING

Sew Pocket to Hat, about 1"/2.5cm above brim. With B, embroider with straight sts around edges of Pocket and around edge of brim.

Weave in ends. •

Next Generation Hat

Easy

SIZES
Child's S (M, L)

MEASUREMENTS
Finished Circumference About 15½ (17, 19)"/39.5 (43, 48.5)cm*
*Will stretch to fit a range of sizes.
Finished Length About 6 (6½, 7)"/15 (16.5, 18)cm

MATERIALS
YARN
LION BRAND® Heartland®, 5oz/142g balls, each approx 251yd/230m (acrylic/rayon)
• 1 ball each in #098 Acadia (A) and #150 Mount Ranier (B)

HOOK
• One size H-8 (5mm) crochet hook, *or size to obtain gauge*

NOTION
• Tapestry needle

GAUGE
14 hdc + 10 rnds = about 4"/10cm.
BE SURE TO CHECK YOUR GAUGE.

NOTE
Hat is worked in the round in one piece.

HAT
With B, ch 54 (60, 64); join with sl st in first ch to form a ring, being careful not to twist ch.
Rnd 1 (RS) Ch 2 (counts as first hdc in this rnd and in all following rnds), hdc in next ch and in each ch around; join with sl st in top of beg ch—54 (60, 64) hdc.
Rnds 2 and 3 Ch 2, hdc in next st and in each st around; join with sl st in top of beg ch.
Fasten off.
Rnd 4 From RS, join A with sl st in same st as joining, ch 2, hdc in next st and in each st around; join with sl st in top of beg ch.
Rnds 5–10 (11, 12) Ch 2, hdc in next st and in each st around; join with sl st in top of beg ch.

SHAPE CROWN
Dec Rnd 1 Ch 2, hdc in next 3 sts, hdc2tog, *hdc in next 4 sts, hdc2tog; rep from * around; join with sl st in top of beg ch—you will have 45 (50, 55) hdc at the end of this rnd.
Dec Rnd 2 Ch 2, hdc in next 2 sts, hdc2tog, *hdc in next 3 sts, hdc2tog; rep from * around; join with sl st in top of beg ch—36 (40, 44) hdc.
Dec Rnd 3 Ch 2, hdc in next st, hdc2tog, *hdc in next 2 sts, hdc2tog; rep from * around; join with sl st in top of beg ch—27 (30, 33) hdc.
Dec Rnd 4 Ch 2, hdc2tog, *hdc in next st, hdc2tog; rep from * around; join with sl st in top of beg ch—18 (20, 22) hdc.
Dec Rnd 5 Ch 1, hdc in next st (beg ch and hdc count as first hdc2tog), *hdc2tog; rep from * around; join with sl st in first hdc—9 (10, 11) hdc.
Fasten off, leaving a long yarn tail. Thread yarn tail through remaining sts and pull to gather. Knot securely.

FINISHING
Weave in ends. •

Town and Country Hat

Easy

SIZE
Finished Circumference About 19"/48.5cm*
*Will stretch to fit a range of sizes.

MATERIALS
YARN
LION BRAND® Hometown®, 5oz/142g balls, each approx 81yd/74m (acrylic)
• 2 balls in #314 Fresno Tweed

HOOK
• One size N-13 (9mm) crochet hook, *or size to obtain gauge*

NOTION
• Tapesetry needle

GAUGE
8 hdc = about 4"/10cm.
BE SURE TO CHECK YOUR GAUGE.

NOTE
Hat band is worked back and forth in rows, then last row is joined to first row to form a ring. The first rnd of Hat is worked across one long side of band.

HAT
BAND
Ch 6.
Row 1 Sc in 2nd ch from hook and in each ch across—5 sc.
Row 2 Ch 1, turn. Working in back loops only, sc in each st across.
Rep Row 2 until piece measures about 19"/48.5cm from beg.

Hold first and last row tog. With sts matching and working through both thicknesses, sl st in each st across to join. Do not fasten off.

BODY
Rnd 1 Ch 1, working in ends of rows across one long side of band, work 36 sc evenly spaced around; join with sl st in first st—36 sts.
Rnds 2–7 Ch 2, (counts as first hdc in this rnd and in all following rnds), hdc in each st around; join with sl st in beg ch.

SHAPE CROWN
Rnd 8 Ch 2, hdc in next st, hdc2tog, *hdc in next 2 sts, hdc2tog; rep from * to end of rnd; join with sl st in beg ch—27 sts at end of this rnd.
Rnd 9 Ch 2, hdc2tog, *hdc in next st, hdc2tog; rep from * to end of rnd; join with sl st in beg ch—18 sts.
Rnd 10 Ch 2, yarn over, insert hook into next st, yarn over, draw up a loop, yarn over, draw through all 3 loops on hook (1 st decreased), hdc2tog around; join with sl st in beg ch—9 sts.
Fasten off, leaving a long yarn tail.
Thread yarn tail through sts of last rnd and pull to gather. Knot securely.

FINISHING
Weave in ends. •

Iconic Cap

Easy

MEASUREMENTS
Finished Circumference About 20"/51cm*
*Will stretch to fit a range of sizes.
Finished Height About 8½"/21.5cm

MATERIALS
YARN
LION BRAND® Touch of Alpaca, 3½oz/100g balls, each approx 207yd/190m (acrylic, alpaca)
- 1 ball in #132 Olive

HOOK
- One size J-10 (6mm) crochet hook, *or size to obtain gauge*

NOTION
- Tapestry needle

GAUGE
11 sc = about 4"/10cm.
BE SURE TO CHECK YOUR GAUGE.

NOTES
1) Ribbing is worked first, back and forth in rows, then stitches are worked across one long edge of ribbing for Cap.
2) Cap is worked in joined rnds.

CAP
RIBBING
Ch 9.
Row 1 Sc in 2nd ch from hook and in each ch across—8 sc.
Row 2 Ch 1, turn, working in front loops only, sc in each st across.
Rep Row 2 until unstretched piece measures about 19"/48.5cm from beg.

BODY
Rnd 1 Ch 1, work 55 sc evenly spaced across one long edge of ribbing; join with sl st in first sc—you will have 55 sc at end of this rnd.
Note Open ends of ribbing will be sewn tog later.
Rnd 2 Ch 1, sc in same st as joining and each st around; join with sl st in first sc.
Rep Rnd 2 until piece measures about 6½"/16.5cm above ribbing.
Fasten off, leaving a long yarn tail. Thread tail into tapestry needle and then weave through sts of last rnd. Pull to close top of Cap. Knot securely.

FINISHING
Sew ends of ribbing tog.
Weave in ends. •

Ridgewood Hat

Easy

MEASUREMENTS
Finished Circumference About 20½"/52cm*
*Will stretch to fit a range of sizes.

MATERIALS
YARN
LION BRAND® Hometown®, 5oz/142g balls, each approx 81yd/74m (acrylic) (6)
- 2 balls in #317 Carson City Tweed

HOOK
- One size P-15 (10mm) crochet hook, *or size to obtain gauge*

NOTION
- Tapestry needle

GAUGE
7 sts = about 4½"/11.5cm over Row 2 of pattern.
BE SURE TO CHECK YOUR GAUGE.

NOTES
1) Hat is worked as a rectangle, back and forth in rows, then seamed.
2) Stitches of the last row are gathered for top of Hat.
3) For those who find a visual helpful, we've included a stitch diagram.

HAT
Ch 34.
Row 1 Sc in 4th ch from hook (3 skipped ch count as dc), *dc in next ch, sc in next ch; rep from * across—you will have 16 dc and 16 sc.
Row 2 Ch 3 (counts as dc), turn, sk first sc, *sc in next dc, dc in next sc; rep from * to beg ch, sc in top of beg ch.
Rep Row 2 until piece measures about 13"/33cm from beg. Fasten off, leaving a long yarn tail. Thread yarn tail into tapestry needle, then through sts of last row. Pull tail to gather top of Hat.
Sew sides tog for back seam of Hat.

FINISHING
Weave in ends. •

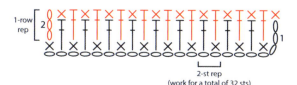

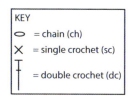

Greenpoint Grunge Cap

Easy

MEASUREMENTS
Finished circumference 20"/51cm*
*Will stretch to fit a range of sizes.

MATERIALS
YARN
LION BRAND® Hometown®, 5oz/142g balls, each approx 81yd/74m (acrylic)
- 1 ball each in #148 Portland Wine (A) and #171 Key Lime (B)

HOOK
- One size P-15 (10mm) crochet hook, *or size to obtain gauge*

NOTIONS
- Stitch marker
- Tapestry needle

GAUGE
9½ dc + 5 rnds = 4"/10cm.
BE SURE TO CHECK YOUR GAUGE.

NOTES
1) Cap is worked in rnds beg at lower edge.
2) Rnds 1–9 are worked in joined rnds with right side facing at all times, do not turn.
3) Rnds 10–12 are worked in continuous rnds (spiral). Do not join and do not turn.
4) Color is changed on every rnd on Rnds 1–10. Drop color not in use to WS of piece and carry it up WS until next needed. Enlarge the dropped loop of the color not in use to ensure that it does not unravel. When returning dropped loop to hook, tighten it around hook slightly. The dropped loop and ch at beg of each rnd should be kept loose enough so that the seam does not become pinched or puckered.

CAP
Beg at lower edge with A, ch 48; taking care not to twist ch, join with sl st in first ch to form a ring. Drop A, but do not fasten off.
Rnd 1 (RS) Draw up a loop of B in same ch as joining, ch 3 (counts as first dc in this rnd and in all following rnds), dc in each ch around; join with sl st in top of beg ch—48 dc at the end of this rnd. Drop B, but do not fasten off.
Rnd 2 Return dropped loop of A to hook, ch 1, working in back loops only, sc in each st around; join with sl st in first sc. Drop A, but do not fasten off.
Note From here on, when instructed to drop a color, always drop the color, but do not fasten off.
Rnd 3 Return dropped loop of B to hook, ch 3, working in back loops only, dc in each st around; join with sl st in top of beg ch. Drop B.
Rnd 4 Rep Rnd 2.
Rnd 5 Return dropped loop of B to hook, ch 3, working in back loops only, dc in next 6 sts, sk next st, *dc in next 7 sts, sk next st; rep from * around; join with sl st in top of beg ch—42 dc. Drop B.
Rnd 6 Rep Rnd 2.
Rnd 7 Return dropped loop of B to hook, ch 3, working in back loops only, dc in next 3 sts, sk next st, *dc in next 6 sts, sk next st; rep from * 4 more times, dc in next 2 sts; join with sl st in top of beg ch—36 dc. Drop B.
Rnd 8 Rep Rnd 2.
Rnd 9 Return dropped loop of B to hook, ch 3, sk next st, working in back loops only, *dc in next 3 sts, sk next st; rep from * to last 2 sts, dc in last 2 sts; join with sl st in top of beg ch—27 dc. Drop B.
Rnd 10 Return dropped loop of A to hook, ch 1, working in back loops only, *sc in next 2 sts, sk next st; rep from *

around; do not join, work in continuous rnds (spiral)—18 sts. Drop A. Place marker for beg of rnd. Move marker up as each rnd is completed.

Rnd 11 Working in back loops only, *sc in next st, sk next st; rep from * around—9 sts.

Rnd 12 Working in back loops only, [sk next st, sc in next st] 4 times, sc in last st—5 sts.

Fasten off, leaving a long yarn tail.

Thread yarn tail through rem sts and pull to gather. Knot securely.

FINISHING

Weave in ends. •

Hat and Mitts

Easy

MEASUREMENTS

HAT
Finished Circumference About 19½"/49.5cm*
*Will stretch to fit a range of sizes.
Finished Height About 11"/28cm

MITTS
Finished Circumference About 7"/18cm
Finished Length About 6"/15cm

MATERIALS

YARN
LION BRAND® Mandala®, 5.3oz/150g balls, each approx 590yd/540m (acrylic) 🔲3🔲
- 1 ball in #201 Unicorn

HOOK
- One size H-8 (5mm) crochet hook, *or size to obtain gauge*

NOTIONS
- One pompom maker
- Tapestry needle

GAUGE
8 V-sts = about 4"/10cm.
BE SURE TO CHECK YOUR GAUGE.

STITCH GLOSSARY
V-st (V-stitch) Work 2 dc in indicated st or sp.

NOTES
1) The Hat is made from a rectangle worked back and forth in rows of V-sts. One end is gathered for top of Hat, the side edges are seamed, and then a pom-pom is tied to top of Hat.
2) For the Mitts, yarn is divided into separate colors.
3) Each Mitt is made from a rectangle worked back and forth in rows of V-sts with planned color changes to make stripes.
4) To change color, work last st of old color to last yarn over. Yarn over with new color and draw through all loops on hook to complete st. Proceed with new color. Fasten off old color.

HAT
Ch 82.
Row 1 Dc in 4th ch from hook (3 skipped ch count as dc), *sk next ch, V-st in next ch; rep from * to last 2 ch, sk next ch, dc in last ch—you will have 38 V-sts and a dc at beg and end of this row.
Row 2 Ch 3 (counts as dc), turn. V-st in sp between dc sts of each V-st across, dc in top of beg ch.
Rep Row 2 until piece measures about 11"/28cm from beg.
Last Row Ch 3 (counts as dc), turn. Dc in sp between dc sts of each V-st across, dc in top of beg ch.
Fasten off, leaving a long tail.

FINISHING
Thread yarn tail into tapestry needle, then through sts of last row. Pull tail to close top of Hat and knot. Sew sides of Hat tog.
Weave in ends.
Following package directions, make a pompom and tie to top of Hat.

MITTS (MAKE 2)
Note Before beginning Mitts, divide rem yarn into 3 separate balls—one each of 3 colors. Use colors in any sequence you like.
With first color yarn, ch 32.

Row 1 Dc in 4th ch from hook (3 skipped ch count as dc), *sk next ch, V-st in next ch; rep from * to last 2 ch, sk next ch, dc in last ch—you will have 13 V-sts and a dc at beg and end of this row.

Rows 2–7 Ch 3 (counts as dc), turn, V-st in sp between dc sts of each V-st across, dc in top of beg ch; change to 2nd color yarn in last st of Row 7.

Rows 8–12 With 2nd color, rep Row 2 five times; change to 3rd color yarn in last st of Row 12.

With 3rd color, rep Row 2 until piece measures about 6"/15cm from beg. Fasten off.

FINISHING

Sew side edges tog, leaving about 1½"/3.5cm unsewn for thumb opening. Weave in ends. •

Slouchy Stripe Hat

Easy

SIZES
Child S (Child M/L, Adult S/M, Adult L)

MEASUREMENTS
Finished Circumference About 16 (18½, 21, 22)"/40.5 (47, 53.5, 56)cm*
*Will stretch to fit a range of sizes.

MATERIALS
YARN

LION BRAND® Wool-Ease® Thick & Quick®, 6oz/170g balls, each approx 106yd/97m (acrylic/wool)
• 1 ball each in #143 Claret (A) and #133 Pumpkin (B)

HOOK
• One size N-13 (9mm) crochet hook, *or size to obtain gauge*

NOTIONS
• Stitch markers
• Tapestry needle

GAUGE
6½ sc = 4/10cm.
BE SURE TO CHECK YOUR GAUGE.

STITCH GLOSSARY
FPdc (front post double crochet) Yarn over, insert hook from front to back then to front, going around post of indicated st, draw up a loop, [yarn over and draw through 2 loops on hook] twice. Skip st behind the FPdc.

NOTES
1) Band is worked in the rnd with RS always facing, do not turn.
2) Hat is worked in rnds, turning at the end of every rnd.
3) To change color, work last st of old color to last yarn over. Yarn over with new color and draw through all loops on hook to complete the st.
4) Do not cut yarn between rnds, just carry unused color up inside of Hat.

HAT
BAND

Note Each dc of Rnd 1 of the Band is worked around (rather than in) a ch, to create a tidy edge.

With A, ch 26 (30, 34, 36). Being careful not to twist, join with sl st in first ch to make a ring.

Rnd 1 Ch 2 (counts as first hdc), dc around (rather than in) next ch, *hdc in next ch, dc around next ch; rep from * around, join with sl st in top of beg ch-2. Place marker for beg of rnd. Move marker up as each rnd is completed—26 (30, 34, 36) sts.

Rnd 2 Ch 2 (counts as first hdc), do NOT turn, FPdc in next dc, *hdc in next hdc, FPdc in next dc; rep from * around, join with sl st in beg ch-2.

For adult sizes only
Rnd 3 Rep Rnd 2.

BODY
Change to B.

Rnd 1 Ch 1, sc in each st around; join with sl st in turning ch.

Rnd 2 Ch 1, turn, sc in each st around; join with sl st in turning ch.

Rep Rnd 2, alternating A and B every 2 rnds, until 12 (12, 14, 14) rnds have been completed.

SHAPE CROWN

Notes 1) Shaping instructions are specific for each size. 2) While working crown shaping, continue to work in stripe sequence of 2 rnds of each color.

Size Child S ONLY

Dec Rnd 1 Ch 1, turn, *sc in each of next 3 sc, sc2tog; rep from * to last st, sc in last st, join with sl st in turning ch—21 sts.
Dec Rnd 2 Ch 1, turn, *sc in each of next 2 sc, sc2tog; rep from * to last st, sc in last st, join with sl st in turning ch—16 sts.
Dec Rnd 3 Ch 1, turn, *sc in next sc, sc2tog; rep from * to last st, sc in last st, join with sl st in turning ch—11 sts.
Dec Rnd 4 Ch 1, turn, *sc2tog; rep from * to last st, sc in last st, join with sl st in turning ch—6 sts.

Size Child M/L ONLY

Dec Rnd 1 Ch 1, turn, *sc in each of next 3 sc, sc2tog; rep from * around, join with sl st in turning ch—24 sts.
Dec Rnd 2 Ch 1, turn, *sc in each of next 2 sc, sc2tog; rep from * around, join with sl st in turning ch—18 sts.
Dec Rnd 3 Ch 1, turn, *sc in next sc, sc2tog; rep from * around, join with sl st in turning ch—12 sts.
Dec Rnd 4 Ch 1, turn, *sc2tog; rep from * around, join with sl st in turning ch—6 sts.

Size Adult S/M ONLY

Dec Rnd 1 Ch 1, turn, *sc in each of next 3 sc, sc2tog; rep from * to last 4 sts, sc in last 2 sts, sc2tog; join with sl st in turning ch—27 sts.
Dec Rnd 2 Ch 1, turn, *sc in each of next 2 sc, sc2tog; rep from * to last 3 sts, sc in next sc, sc2tog, join with sl st in turning ch—20 sts.
Dec Rnd 3 Ch 1, turn, *sc in next sc, sc2tog; rep from * to last 2 sts, sc in last 2 sts, join with sl st in turning ch—14 sts.
Dec Rnd 4 Ch 1, turn, *sc2tog around, join with sl st in turning ch—7 sts.

Size Adult L ONLY

Dec Rnd 1 Ch 1, turn, *sc in each of next 3 sc, sc2tog; rep from * to last st, sc in last st, join with sl st in turning ch—29 sts.
Dec Rnd 2 Ch 1, turn, *sc in each of next 2 sc, sc2tog; rep from * to last st, sc in last st, join with sl st in turning ch—22 sts.
Dec Rnd 3 Ch 1, turn, *sc in next sc, sc2tog; rep from * to last st, sc in last st, join with sl st in turning ch—15 sts.
Dec Rnd 4 Ch 1, turn, *sc2tog; rep from * to last st, sc in last st, join with sl st in turning ch—8 sts.
Fasten off, leaving a long yarn tail. Flatten Hat, and with yarn tail, sew top closed.

FINISHING

Weave in ends. •

The Romantic Hat

Easy

MEASUREMENTS
Finished Circumference About 19"/48.5cm*
*Will stretch to fit a range of sizes.
Finished Height (excluding Earflaps) About 7½"/19cm

MATERIALS
YARN
LION BRAND® Vanna's Choice®, 3½oz/100g balls, each approx 170yd/156m (acrylic)
- 1 ball each in #180 Cranberry (A) and #112 Raspberry (B)

HOOK
- One size J-10 (6mm) crochet hook, *or size to obtain gauge*

NOTION
- Tapestry needle

GAUGE
12 sc + 16 rnds = about 4"/10cm.
BE SURE TO CHECK YOUR GAUGE.

ADJUSTABLE RING
Wrap yarn around index finger. Insert hook into ring on finger, yarn over and draw up a loop. Carefully slip ring from finger and work the stitches of Rnd 1 (as instructed) into the ring. When Rnd 1 is complete, gently but firmly, pull tail to tighten center of ring.

NOTES
1) Hat is worked in joined and turned rnds, beg at lower edge.
2) Work is turned at the end of each round, rather than worked with RS always facing, so that the sts of the Hat will match the sts of the Earflaps.
3) Color is changed to create stripes. To change color, fasten off old color and join new color as instructed.
4) Heart-shaped Earflaps are worked separately, and sewn to Hat.
5) If you find it difficult to join the beg ch into a ring without twisting the ch, Rnd 1 can be worked as a row, then joined into a rnd, as follows: Leaving a long beg tail, ch 57, sc in 2nd ch from hook and in each ch across; join with sl st in first sc—56 sc. Use beg tail to sew gap at base of first row closed. Proceed to Rnd 2.

HAT
With A, ch 56, taking care not to twist ch, join with sl st in first ch to form ring.
Rnd 1 (RS) Ch 1, sc in same ch as joining, sc in each ch around, join with sl st in first sc—56 sts.
Rnds 2–6 Ch 1, turn. Sc in each st around, join with sl st in first sc. Fasten off A.
Rnd 7 From RS, join B with sl st in same st as joining, sc same st and in each st around, join with sl st in first sc.
Rnd 8 Ch 1, turn, sc in each st around; join with sl st in first sc. Fasten off B.
Rnd 9 With A, rep Rnd 7.
Rnds 10–12 With A, rep Rnd 8. Fasten off A.
Rnds 13 and 14 With B, rep Rnds 7 and 8. Fasten off B.
Rnds 15 and 16 With A, rep Rnds 7 and 8. Fasten off A.
Rnd 17 With B, rep Rnd 7.
Rnds 18–20 With B, rep Rnd 8. Fasten off B.

SHAPE CROWN
Rnd 1 (RS From RS, join A with sl st in same st as joining, sc in same st and in next 4 sts, sc2tog, *sc in next 5 sts, sc2tog; rep from * around, join with sl st in first sc—48 sts.

Rnd 2 With A, ch 1, turn, sc in each st around; join with sl st in first sc. Fasten off A.

Rnd 3 From RS, join B with sl st in same st as joining, sc in same st and in next 3 sts, sc2tog, *sc in next 4 sts, sc2tog; rep from * around, join with sl st in first sc—40 sts.

Rnd 4 With B, ch 1, turn, sc in each st around, join with sl st in first sc.

Rnd 5 With B, ch 1, turn, *sc in next 3 sts, sc2tog; rep from * around, join with sl st in first sc—32 sts.

Rnd 6 With B, ch 1, turn, sc in each st around, join with sl st in first sc.

Rnd 7 With B, ch 1, turn, *sc in next 2 sts, sc2tog; rep from * around, join with sl st in first sc—24 sts.

Rnd 8 With B, ch 1, turn, sc in each st around, join with sl st in first sc. Fasten off B.

Rnd 9 From RS, join A with sl st in same st as joining, sc in same st, sc2tog, *sc in next st, sc2tog; rep from * around; join with sl st in first sc—16 sts.

Rnd 10 With A, ch 1, turn, sc2tog around, join with sl st in first sc—8 sts.

Fasten off A, leaving a long yarn tail for sewing. Use yarn tail to sew top of Hat closed.

HEART EARFLAP (MAKE 2)

With B, make an adjustable ring.

Rnd 1 (RS) Ch 1, work 6 sc in ring; join with sl st in first sc—6 sts.

Rnd 2 Ch 1, 2 sc in each st around; join with sl st in first sc—12 sts.

Rnd 3 Ch 1, *sc in next st, 2 sc in next st; rep from * around; join with sl st in first sc—18 sts.

Rnd 4 Ch 1, sc in next st, 2 sc in next st, sc in next st, (hdc, dc) in next st, 2 dc in next st, dc in next st, sl st in next st, dc in next st, 2 dc in next st, (dc, hdc) in next st, sc in next st, 2 sc in next st, sc in next 3 sts, 2 sc in next st, sc in next 2 sts; join with sl st in first sc—25 sts.

Rnd 5 Ch 1, sc in next 3 sts, (hdc, dc) in next st, 2 dc in each of next 3 sts, dc in next 2 sts, sl st in next st, dc in next 2 sts, 2 dc in each of next 3 sts, (dc, hdc) in next st, sc in next 6 sts, ch 2, sl st in 2nd ch from hook (picot made), sc in next 3 sts; join with sl st in first sc—33 sts and 1 picot.

Fasten off.

FINISHING
Earflaps

Place one Heart on each side of Hat, overlapping about 1"/2.5cm of lower edge of Hat and with point of Heart facing down and sew in place.

Braids

Cut 3 strands of A and 3 strands of B, each about 30"/76cm long. Thread all 6 strands through picot at point of Heart Earflap and fold in half for 12 strands. Divide strands into 3 groups of 4 strands each and braid for 12"/30.5cm. Tie end of braid in a knot to secure. Trim ends to about 1"/2.5cm long.

Rep for braid on other Earflap.

Weave in ends. •

First Fall Crochet Hat

Beginner

MEASUREMENTS
Finished circumference About 18"/46cm*
*Will stretch to fit a range of sizes

MATERIALS
YARN
LION BRAND® Vanna's Choice®, 3½oz/100g balls, each approx 170yd/156m (acrylic)
- 1 ball in #109 Colonial Blue

HOOK
- One size J-10 (6mm) crochet hook, *or size to obtain gauge*

NOTIONS
- Tapestry needle
- One faux-fur pompom

GAUGE
12 sc + 15 rows = 4"/10cm.
BE SURE TO CHECK YOUR GAUGE.

NOTE
The Pom is tied to the top of the hat.

HAT
Leaving a long tail, chain 55.
Row 1 Sc in 2nd chain from hook and each chain across—54 sts.
Row 2 Ch 1, turn, sc in each st across.
Rep Row 2 until piece measures about 9"/23cm from beg. Fasten off, leaving a long tail.

FINISHING
Thread tail into tapestry needle, then sew in and out along last row. Pull (like a drawstring) to gather top of hat and knot. Sew seam. Weave in ends.
Attach pompom to top of hat. •

Urban Minimalist Hat

Easy

MEASUREMENT
Finished Circumference About 18"/45.5cm*
*Will stretch to fit a range of sizes.
Finished Height About 12"/30.5cm

MATERIALS
YARN
LION BRAND® Vanna's Choice®, 3½oz/100g balls, each approx 170yd/156m (acrylic)
- 1 ball in #151 Charcoal Grey (A)

HOOK
- One size J-10 (6mm) crochet hook, *or size to obtain gauge*

NOTION
- Tapestry needle

GAUGE
12 dc = about 4"/10cm.
BE SURE TO CHECK YOUR GAUGE.

NOTE
Hat is crocheted and then seamed.

HAT
Ch 55.
Row 1 Sc in 2nd ch from hook and in each ch across—at end of Row 1 you will have 54 sc.
Rows 2–4 Ch 1, turn, sc in each st across.
Row 5 Ch 3 (counts as first dc), turn, sk first st, dc in next st and in each st across.
Rep last row until piece measures about 11"/28cm from beg.
Dec Row Ch 3 (does not count as first dc), turn, dc2tog across.
Next Row Ch 3 (counts as first dc), turn, sk first st, dc in next st and in each st across.
Fasten off, leaving a long yarn tail. Thread tail through rem sts and pull to gather. Knot securely.

FINISHING
Seam sides of piece to make Hat.
Weave in ends. •

Warmest Regards Hat

Easy

MEASUREMENTS
Finished Circumference About 18"/45.5cm
Finished Height About 9"/23cm

MATERIALS
YARN
LION BRAND® Schitt's Creek, 7oz/200g balls, each approx 372yd/340m (acrylic) (4)
• 1 ball in #153 Black Crow

HOOK
• One size J-10 (6mm) crochet hook, *or size to obtain gauges*

NOTIONS
• Tapestry needle
• Purchased pompom

GAUGES
• 10 hdc = about 3"/7.5cm.
• 10 sc + 10 rows = about 3"/7.5cm.
BE SURE TO CHECK YOUR GAUGE.

STITCH GLOSSARY
FPdc (Front Post dc) Yarn over, insert hook from front to back then to front, going around post of indicated st, draw up a loop, [yarn over and draw through 2 loops on hook] twice. Sk top of st behind FPdc.
sc-blo (sc in back loop only) Insert hook in back loop only of indicated st and draw up a loop, yarn over and draw through 2 loops on hook.

NOTES
1) Ribbing is worked first, as a rectangle and back and forth in rows.
2) Ribbing is folded, then stitches for body of Hat are worked across long edge of folded ribbing.
3) Decreases are worked to shape the top of Hat, then a purchased pompom is sewn on.

HAT
RIBBING
Leaving a long beg yarn tail, ch 17.
Row 1 Working in back bumps only, sc in 2nd ch from hook in each ch across—you will have 16 sc in this row.
Rows 2–60 Ch 1, turn, sc in first st, sc-blo in next 14 sts, sc in last st.
Do not fasten off.

BODY
Fold ribbing in half lengthwise, bringing long edges tog, to make a double layer.
Rnd 1 (RS) Ch 1, working through both thicknesses, work 60 hdc evenly spaced along long edge of folded ribbing; join with sl st in first st to form a ring—60 hdc.

NOTES
1) Body of Hat is now worked in joined rnds with RS always facing out.
2) Do not turn at beg of rnds.
3) Work first st of each rnd in same st as joining sl st, unless otherwise instructed.

Rnds 2–16 Ch 1, hdc in first 2 sts, FPdc around each of next 2 sts, *hdc in next 4 sts, FPdc around each of next 2 sts; rep from * to last 2 sts, hdc in last 2 sts; join with sl st in first st.

SHAPE CROWN
Rnd 17 Ch 1, hdc in first 2 sts, FPdc around each of next 2 sts, *hdc2tog, hdc in next 2 sts, FPdc around each of

next 2 sts; rep from * to last 2 sts; hdc2tog; join with sl st in first st—50 hdc.

Rnd 18 Ch 1, hdc in first 2 sts, FPdc around each of next 2 sts, *hdc in next 3 sts, FPdc around each of next 2 sts; rep from * to last st; hdc in last st; join with sl st in first st.

Rnd 19 Ch 1, hdc2tog, FPdc around each of next 2 sts, *hdc in next st, hdc2tog, FPdc around each of next 2 sts; rep from * to last st; hdc in last st; join with sl st in first st —40 hdc.

Rnd 20 Ch 1, hdc in first st, FPdc around each of next 2 sts, *hdc in next 2 sts, FPdc around each of next 2 sts; rep from * to last st; hdc in last st; join with sl st in first st.

Rnd 21 Ch 1, sk first st, FPdc around each of next 2 sts, *hdc2tog, FPdc around each of next 2 sts; rep from * to last st; hdc in last st; join with sl st in first st—30 hdc.

Rnd 22 Ch 1, *FPdc around each of next 2 sts, hdc in next st; rep from * around; join with sl st in first st. Fasten off, leaving a long tail. Thread tail through sts of last rnd and pull to close opening at top of Hat. Knot securely.

FINISHING

Sew pompom to top of Hat.
Use long beg tail to sew ends of ribbing tog.
Weave in ends. •

Toboggan Hat

Easy

SIZES
Child S (Child M/L, Adult S/M, Adult L)

MEASUREMENTS
Finished Circumference About 17 (19, 21, 23)"/43 (48.5, 53.5, 58.5)cm*
*Will stretch to fit a range of sizes.
Finished Height (excluding earflaps) About 5 (6, 7½, 8)"/12.5 (15, 19, 20.5)cm

MATERIALS
YARN
LION BRAND® Wool-Ease® Thick & Quick®, 6oz/170g balls, each approx 106yd/97m (acrylic/wool) (6)
- 1 ball in #110 Navy

HOOK
- One size P-15 (10mm) crochet hook, *or size to obtain gauge*

NOTIONS
- Pompom maker
- Tapestry needle

GAUGE
6½ sc = about 4"/10cm.
BE SURE TO CHECK YOUR GAUGE.

NOTES
1) Hat is worked in joined and turned rnds, beginning at top of Hat.
2) Earflaps are worked back and forth in rows, onto lower edge of Hat.

HAT
Ch 2.
Rnd 1 Work 7 sc in 2nd ch from hook; join with sl st in first sc—7 sts.
Rnd 2 Ch 1, turn, 2 sc in each st around; join with sl st in first sc—14 sts at the end of this rnd.
Rnd 3 Ch 1, turn, *2 sc in next st, sc in next st; rep from * around; join with sl st in first sc—21 sts.
Rnd 4 Ch 1, turn, *2 sc in next st, sc in each of next 2 sts; rep from * around; join with sl st in first sc—28 sts.

Sizes Child M/L (Adult S/M, Adult L) ONLY
Rnd 5 Ch 1, turn, *2 sc in next st, sc in next 13 (3, 2) sts; rep from * 1 (5, 7) more time(s), sc to end of rnd; join with sl st in first sc—30 (34, 36) sts.

All Sizes
Next Rnd Ch 1, turn, sc in each st around; join with sl st in first sc.
Rep last rnd until piece measures 5 (6, 7½, 8)"/12.5 (15, 19, 20.5)cm from beg.
Note Beg with next row, work back and forth in rows.
Next Row Ch 1, turn, sc in next 19 (20, 23, 24) sts; leave rem 9 (10, 11, 12) sts unworked for front of Hat.

FIRST EARFLAP
Row 1 (RS) Ch 1, turn, sc in first st, sc2tog, sc in next 4 (5, 6, 6) sts; leave rem 12 (12, 14, 15) sts unworked for back of Hat and right earflap.
Continue on these 6 (7, 8, 8) sts for first earflap ONLY.
Row 2 Ch 1, turn, sc2tog, sc in each st to last 2 sts, sc2tog—4 (5, 6, 6) sts.
Row 3 Ch 1, turn, sc in each st across.
Rows 4–5 (5, 7, 7) Rep last 2 rows—2 (3, 2, 2) sts rem. Fasten off.

SECOND EARFLAP

Row 1 (RS) From RS, sk first 5 (5, 5, 6) unworked sts following first earflap, join A with sc in next st, sc in next 3 (4, 5, 5) sts, sc2tog, sc in next st—6 (7, 8, 8) sts for 2nd earflap.

Rows 2–5 (5, 7, 7) Work same as Rows 2–5 (5, 7, 7) of first earflap—2 (3, 2, 2) sts rem.

Do not fasten off, do not turn.

FINISHING

Edging

Next Rnd Ch 1, work sc evenly spaced around edge of Hat. Fasten off.

Following package directions, make a medium pompom.

Tie pompom to top of Hat.

Weave in ends. •

Simply Basic Hat, Scarf, and Gloves Set

Easy

MEASUREMENTS

HAT
Finished Circumference About 18"/45.5cm*
*Will stretch to fit a range of sizes.

SCARF
About 5½ x 60"/14 x 152.5cm, excluding fringe

GLOVES
Finished Circumference About 8"/20.5cm
Finished Length About 7½"/19cm

MATERIALS

YARN
LION BRAND® Heartland®, 5oz/142g balls, each approx 251yd/230m (acrylic/rayon) (4)
- 2 balls in #098 Acadia

HOOKS
- One size I-9 (5.5mm) crochet hook, *or size to obtain gauge*
- One size G-6 (4.25 mm) crochet hook
- One size J-10 (6mm) crochet hook

NOTION
- Tapestry needle

GAUGE
Five 2-dc groups = about 4"/10cm with size I-9 (5.5mm) hook.
BE SURE TO CHECK YOUR GAUGE.

NOTES
1) Hat and Gloves are worked from top down.
2) Scarf trim is a chained fringe.

HAT

With size I-9 (5.5 mm) hook, ch 4, join with sl st in first ch to form a ring.

Rnd 1 Ch 1, work 10 sc in ring, join with sl st in beg sc —10 sc.

Rnd 2 Ch 4 (counts as dc, ch 1), sk first st, [dc in next st, ch 1] 9 times, join with sl st in 3rd ch of beg ch-4 —10 ch-1 sps at end of rnd.

Rnd 3 Sl st in last ch-1 sp of Rnd 2, ch 3, dc in same sp, [ch 1, 2 dc in next ch-1 sp] 9 times, ch 1, join with sl st in top of beg ch-3—20 dc and 10 ch-1 sps.

Increase Rnd 4 Sl st in last ch-1 sp of Rnd 3, ch 3, dc in same ch-sp, (ch 1, 2 dc) in next ch-1 sp, *(ch 1, 2 dc) in 2nd dc of next 2-dc group, *[ch 1, 2 dc in next ch-sp] twice; rep from * 3 times, ch 1, 2 dc in 2nd dc of last 2-dc group, ch 1, join with sl st in top of beg ch-3—15 ch-1 sps.

Rnd 5 Sl st in last ch-1 sp of Rnd 4, ch 3, dc in same sp, ch 1, [2 dc in next ch-sp, ch 1] 14 times, join with sl st in top of beg ch-3—15 ch-1 sps.

Increase Rnd 6 Sl st in last ch-1 sp of Rnd 5, ch 3, dc in same sp, *ch 1, 2 dc in 2nd dc of next 2-dc group, [ch 1, 2 dc in next ch-1 sp] twice; rep from * around, ch 1, join with sl st in top of beg ch-3—22 ch-1 sps.

Rnd 7 Sl st in last ch-1 sp of Rnd 6, ch 3, dc in same sp, [ch 1, 2 dc in next sp] 21 times, ch 1, join with sl st in top of beg ch-3—22 ch-1 sps.

Rnds 8–17 Rep Rnd 7.

Rnd 18 Ch 1, sc in each dc and ch-sp around, join with sl st in top of beg sc—66 sc.

Rnd 19 Ch 2 (counts as first hdc), working in back loops only, hdc in next sc and in each sc around, join with sl st in top of beg ch-2.

Rnd 20 (WS) Ch 2 (counts as first hdc), turn, working through both loops, hdc in next hdc and in each hdc around, join with sl st in top of beg ch-2.
Fasten off. Weave in ends.

Simply Basic Hat, Scarf, and Gloves Set

SCARF

With size J-10 (6mm) hook, ch 25, leaving a 30"/76cm beg yarn tail.

Row 1 Dc in 4th ch from hook, [ch 1, sk 2 ch, 2 dc in next ch] 7 times.

Row 2 Ch 4 (counts as dc, ch-1), turn, [2 dc in next ch-sp, ch 1] 7 times, dc in top of turning ch.

Row 3 Ch 3, turn, dc in first ch-sp, [ch 1, 2 dc in next ch-space] 7 times.

Rep Rows 2 and 3 until piece measures about 60"/152cm from beg. Fasten off, leaving a 30"/76cm yarn tail.

CHAINED FRINGE

Cut 26 strands of yarn, each 60"/152cm long. Fold strand in half. Use crochet hook to draw fold through edge of Scarf, forming a loop. Pull ends of strand through this loop. Pull to tighten.

Attach 13 strands evenly spaced across each end of Scarf. Starting at loop end with size G-6 (4.25mm) hook, ch each strand tightly, then fasten off.

GLOVES (MAKE 2)

With size G-6 (4.25mm) hook, beg at top of hand, ch 30, join with sl st in beg ch to form a ring.

Rnd 1 Ch 3 (counts as dc), dc in first ch, [ch 1, sk 2 ch, 2 dc in next ch] 9 times, ch 1, join with sl st in top of beg ch-3.

Rnd 2 Sl st in last ch-1 sp of Rnd 1, ch 3, dc in same sp, [ch 1, 2 dc in next ch-1 sp] 9 times, ch 1, join with sl st in top of beg ch-3.

Rnds 3 and 4 Rep Rnd 2.

THUMB OPENING

Note Work back and forth in rows, leaving sts unworked for thumb.

Row 5 (WS) Rep Row 3 of Scarf.

Row 6 Rep Row 2 of Scarf.

Row 7 Rep Row 3 of Scarf.

Joining (WS) Ch 8, join with sl st in top of beg ch-3. Return to working in rnds with RS facing.

Rnd 1 Ch 3, turn, dc in first ch, [ch 1, sk 2 ch, 2 dc in next ch] twice, sk last ch, [ch 1, 2 dc in ch-1 sp] 7 times, ch 1, join with sl st in top of beg ch-3—10 ch-1 sps.

Rnd 2 Sl st in last ch-1 sp of Rnd 1, ch 3, dc in same sp, [ch 1, 2 dc in next ch-sp] 11 times, ch 1, join with sl st in top of beg ch-3.

Rnds 3–6 Rep Rnd 2.

Change to size I-9 (5.5mm) hook.

Rnds 7 and 8 Rep Rnds 18 and 19 of Hat—30 sts. Fasten off.

With RS facing and size G-6 (4.25mm) hook, join yarn with sl st to top edge of Glove

Rnd 1 Ch 1, work 30 sc evenly spaced around, join with sl st in first sc.

Rnd 2 Ch 2 (counts as hdc), hdc in next st and in each st around.

Fasten off.

FINISHING

Edging for Thumb Opening

With the RS facing and size G-6 (4.25mm) hook, join yarn with sl st to edge of thumb opening.

Rnd 1 Ch 1, work 22 sc evenly spaced around, join with sl st in first sc.

Rnd 2 Ch 1, working in back loops only, sc in each st around.

Fasten off.

Weave in ends. •